HOW
TO
WIN
WORK

© Jan Knikker, 2021

Published by RIBA Publishing, 66 Portland Place, London, W1B 1AD

ISBN 978-1-85946-932-3

The right/s of Jan Knikker to be identified as the Author of this Work has been asserted in accordance with the Copyright, Designs and Patents Act 1988 sections 77 and 78.

All rights reserved. No part of this publication may be reproduced, stored in a retrieval system, or transmitted, in any form or by any means, electronic, mechanical, photocopying, recording or otherwise, without prior permission of the copyright owner.

British Library Cataloguing-in-Publication Data
A catalogue record for this book is available from the British Library.

Commissioning Editor: Elizabeth Webster
Assistant Editor: Clare Holloway
Production: Jane Rogers
Designed and typeset by Sara Miranda Icaza
Printed and bound by Short Run Press, Exeter
Cover image: Sara Miranda Icaza

While every effort has been made to check the accuracy and quality of the information given in this publication, neither the Author nor the Publisher accept any responsibility for the subsequent use of this information, for any errors or omissions that it may contain, or for any misunderstandings arising from it.

www.ribapublishing.com

HOW TO WIN WORK

JAN KNIKKER

RIBA ♯ **Publishing**

TABLE OF CONTENTS

VI	Foreword: Dispatch from the 'dark side'	
IX	About the Author	
1	**1.** How we are supposed to work for free	
5	**2.** We can do better	
8	**3.** To specialise or not to specialise?	
13	**4.** Marketing: a dirty word in architectual circles	
14	**5.** Mission and vision	
17	**6.** Branding and company culture	
21	**PUBLIC RELATIONS**	
22	**7.** 'If I was down to my last dollar, I would spend it on PR'	
24	7.1 Writing a marketing strategy	
27	**8.** The office is your business card	
30	**9.** Your website: your online shop window	
34	**10.** Your work amid a changing media landscape	
36	10.1 Print media	
40	10.2 Online media	
42	10.3 Social media	
46	10.4 Television	
49	10.5 Vlogs and podcasts	
51	10.6 Crisis communication and the outreach that might prevent it	
57	10.7 Other media	
58	**11.** Lectures	
64	**12.** Awards	
66	**13.** Your product in the picture	
66	13.1 The drawing	
71	13.2 The render	
79	13.3 Collages and hand drawings	
84	13.4 Talking to clients: the project text and press release	
88	13.5 The model	
91	**14.** The built project	
95	**15.** The project book	
98	**16.** Exhibitions	
102	**17.** Prioritising	

105 BUSINESS DEVELOPMENT

- 106 **18.** Business development, the direct way to win new work
- 108 **19.** Client relationships: a personal 'click' or a financial agreement?
- 112 **20.** Who is your client and how do you approach them?
- 115 **21.** Just do it
- 117 **22.** Going abroad
- 123 **23.** Fairs
- 127 **24.** How to calculate a fee
- 132 **25.** Contracts: managing risks and keeping promises
- 137 **26.** It's not easy being green
- 141 **27.** The pitch
- 145 **28.** Broadening your portfolio
- 147 **29.** Planning workflow
- 150 **30.** Collaborations
- 153 **31.** Learning from others
- 156 **32.** Styles
- 159 **33.** Ethics for architects
- 162 **34.** Suing your client
- 164 **35.** Spam and fraud
- 165 **36.** Crisis

169 CASE STUDIES

- 170 **1.** shedkm – Hazel Rounding
- 173 **2.** MgMaStudio – Mathew Giles and Matthew Ashton
- 177 **3.** Studio MUTT – James Crawford
- 181 **4.** Coffey Architects – Phil Coffey
- 185 **5.** DMA – David Miller
- 189 **6.** Feilden Fowles – Edmund Fowles
- 194 **7.** Turner Works – Carl Turner
- 199 **8.** Powerhouse Company – Nanne de Ru

- 202 Acknowledgements
- 203 Image credits
- 204 Index
- 206 Endnotes

FOREWORD:
DISPATCH FROM THE 'DARK SIDE'

This book aims to help you address the noted gaps in your architectural education: explicitly, marketing and entrepreneurial skills. It is certainly true that you can develop these in practice when you pursue them authentically, as you endeavour to make them a holistic and integrated part of the philosophy of your work.

Marketing for a small business is not an exact science, so I attempt to provide general advice for architects, which is not hard and fast. A few years ago, I advised Shift A+U, then a young practice, to leverage the immense power of the render; however, they despised renders as a medium, so they decided to use (more often than not) collages (Figure 0.1). I would not advise this, but they pushed through, and now they are very successful with the collage as a communication tool, even for commercial projects. Collages are very much in vogue. Using renders is more effective in many settings, but Shift A+U considered this standard form of communication practice,

Figure 0.1 *A collage by Shift A+U, Rotterdam. Instead of renders, Shift A+U have successfully deviated from common visualisation with collages.*

and made a deliberate choice to move away from it. To that end, the advice I present in this book can very well be a means of analysing how others do it, and then finding your own unique way of approaching marketing, most suitable for your practice.

Even though I sell (yes, that's marketing) architecture, I could never sell anything I dislike. I believe in the power of being authentic when it comes to marketing, so in this book I also offer a few observations about ethics and sustainability. Architecture by nature is a discipline that can make an enormous difference to the social and sustainable functioning of society. Architecture is the first priority, and marketing the puzzle of determining how best to sell it.

This book began as a lecture when the RIBA's Helen Castle kindly invited me to share some business insights at the 2017 RIBA Smart Practice Conference in Bristol. Helen then invited me to write this book as a practical and accessible guide to marketing for small and mid-size architecture practices. I started writing while travelling, crouched in aeroplanes ('Would you mind not tapping so hard on your laptop? My entire chair shakes...'), and then finalised the book long before my deadline, due to the coronavirus lockdown's strange gift of time. The looming financial consequences of this particular crisis perhaps make this book even more relevant. With it, I aim to provide my insights into how architects can use marketing to maintain and grow their business.

I initially began my career as a journalist, but soon moved to the 'dark side' (marketing!), which I have now practised for over two decades, first for OMA and currently for MVRDV. At MVRDV, they have even made me a partner, the only one who does not bear the architect title. The advantage to not being an architect is that I bring into balance the expectations of clients, the press and the architects. This translation effort is my chief objective in writing this book: how can you transform something as complex as an architectural drawing into a clear argument and an attractive proposal for someone who has not studied architecture?

Although it is a guilty pleasure of mine to make a few jokes about architects, I want to take this moment to emphasise that I have the greatest respect for you and your discipline. Architects perform on many different levels, touching on so many different disciplines and managing extreme complexity.

You are true *homo universalis*, and take on the challenges of solving all kinds of issues and social ills far outside the realm of architecture itself.

During the writing of this book, I interviewed a number of practices which all have an inspiring story to share about the way they have approached marketing. It is more than generous of them to share their trade secrets and I am certain it will prove invaluable.

If you want to share more insights – perhaps how you have successfully approached challenges and found unique ways to market your work – please feel free to connect with me on LinkedIn or your preferred social media channel.

Jan Knikker

ABOUT THE AUTHOR

Partner and Director of Strategy at MVRDV, Jan Knikker (Bad Soden Ts, 1972) joined MVRDV in 2008, just as the practice had begun to face the consequences of the global financial crisis. Prior to this, Knikker shaped OMA's public image for nearly a decade, after having first begun his career as a journalist. Knikker drives business development and public relations efforts at MVRDV, spearheading a large and dynamic studio that also includes the practice's visualisation capacity. He also leads MVRDV's branding efforts, and the practice's expansion into new markets, by supporting its ambition to generate solutions to global challenges through a multifaceted approach to architecture and urbanism.

Knikker regularly lectures at international, commercial and academic venues in Germany (Polis Convention, Stiftung Baukultur), the UK (RIBA), Israel (CTBUH, Bezalel, TAU), Colombia (Universidad Nacional, UTADEO), Austria (MAK), Australia (RMIT), Malaysia (UCSI) and many

Figure 0.2 *A selection of the author's conference, trade fair and visitor badges: during sales activities we are being judged and labelled.*

other notable venues (Figure 0.2). In addition to his extensive public relations work, Knikker has written and contributed to numerous MVRDV publications and exhibitions, including MVRDV Buildings with founding partners Jacob van Rijs and Nathalie de Vries. Deputy editor of *Domus* in 2019 (with Winy Maas as guest editor), he also regularly contributes to a range of architectural magazines. He is a member of the HNI Heritage Network and the Gestaltungsbeirat (Design Advisory Board) of the City of Wiesbaden, led the online design magazine *Dafne*, and from 2007 to 2011 was a member of the International Projects Advisory Board of the Netherlands Architecture Fund. Jan lives with his husband and two sons in the Netherlands.

About the editor that turned Denglish into English

Copywriter at MVRDV, Jessica Cullen (Calgary, 1977) leverages her diverse background in architectural design, creative writing and education to help architectural competition teams translate complex design concepts into clear and compelling narratives. Prior to joining MVRDV in 2019, Cullen worked in business development at Mecanoo, and was instrumental to tenders for such notable projects as the Manchester Engineering Campus Development, the Oldham Coliseum Theatre, Peabody's Thamesmead Regeneration, the NYPL Mid-Manhattan Campus Development, Washington DC's Martin Luther King Jr. Memorial Library renovation and the Lo Recabarren master plan in Santiago, Chile.

A multidisciplinarian and serial hobbyist, Cullen completed her Master of Architecture at the University of Calgary, after having completed her Master of Fine Arts in creative writing (stage play) at the University of British Columbia, and having been a high school English and drama teacher in Vancouver and Nanaimo for over six years. Her thirst for knowledge and new adventures led to her architectural studies, to studies abroad in Adelaide, Australia, and Los Angeles, US, and ultimately to her move to the Netherlands to work at Mecanoo in 2013, and MVRDV thereafter.

CHAPTER 1.
HOW WE ARE SUPPOSED TO WORK FOR FREE

Does this situation sound familiar? At a birthday party, a fellow architect boasts about an exciting new project they have recently acquired. Upon further enquiry, they reveal that – in fact – they slaved over a concept sketch or perhaps managed to coax their client into a commission with a free design to secure the project. These rather intensive and resource-exhaustive periods of unpaid work are not unusual for architecture practices. Yet architecture is not the only discipline to suffer this. It is a scenario common to other creative industries, such as advertising or fashion. Sometimes, working for free can prove a useful strategy to acquire significant long-term projects. It also gives both parties an opportunity to 'test drive' the working dynamic. Nevertheless, it renders the creative work produced worthless. Most egregious is the fact that designers wilfully subject themselves to this exploitation. By surrendering time, energy and resources without pay, designers reinforce the widely held, but very wrong, assumption that creativity and ideas are free.

The infamous Guggenheim Helsinki competition of 2014 is perhaps the most striking example of the devaluation of the architectural idea (Figure 1.1). Some 1,715 architecture teams submitted complex and creative designs

Figure 1.1 *MLBS Architects' Guggenheim Helsinki proposal, one of 1,715.*

without payment for time and talent. Assuming each practice worked 200 hours on their designs and that these hours were each worth £60, this adds up to an investment of over £20.5 million for a project that may never be realised.

When Sheela Maini Søgaard started at Bjarke Ingels Group as chief financial officer, the practice was overextended by unpaid work. She immediately put an end to this, with the intervention of common sense: 'She got them paid. Recognising that the architecture industry was rife with free work, Søgaard brought what Ingels calls a "f*** you, pay me" attitude.' According to the Danish starchitect, Søgaard introduced a sense of business that did not kill creativity but, on the contrary, she was essential in creating an 'uplifting atmosphere conducive to creativity'.[1]

However, for many practices, this is an enviable position to be in. It takes time, dedication and discipline to establish this attitude. Many architects feel pressured into a competition because there is always a fellow architect willing to work for free, especially if there is the possibility of an eventual commission. In general, UK-based architects interviewed for this book reported that they were not willing to work without pay. Although more than a few uttered the caveat 'unless…'. All things considered, it is entirely understandable that 'that one project' or 'that one competition' is so compelling and prestigious as to justify working without a commission.

As a creative profession, architects are often the first to see the potential of a given project. Enthusiasm quickly outpaces the business case, and they want to design instantly. For some architects, this initial unpaid work can form an integral component of the acquisition process. The savvy players of other disciplines negotiate terms with their clients as a matter of course. Architects should adopt this same attitude. Even if negotiation is a loathsome process, establishing payment terms for work is without question entirely justified. Cafés do not hand out free cappuccinos, with the assumption you might purchase a second if the first entices you. The customer receives their cappuccino upon paying for it. Architects should be paid for their work.

PRACTICAL TIPS FOR MANAGING UNPAID WORK

Take time to calculate your chances. Architectural competitions vary in their structure, often according to the country in which they are taking place, but more often than not they have poor conditions. In Germany, for example, architectural competitions often consist of 30 practices competing, with only the first 5 receiving a (small) fee. The remaining 25 effectively work without compensation, producing the same amount of work as those shortlisted. One means of countering this is being selective and beginning with a worst-case, rather than best-case, scenario. Consider how much of a loss you are prepared to suffer and make a probability calculation. A 1 out of 30 chance of winning is a very poor statistic (just over a 3% chance of success), while 1 out of 4 (25%) is a fair chance. Surprisingly, a lost competition can generate a positive PR boost. However, statistics also come into play here. The 4 finalists' projects are more likely to be published than the remaining 30. In the case of the ill-fated Guggenheim Helsinki competition, many practices experienced a positive surge in PR by publishing their project. Committing to a clear and decisive strategy facilitates impartial decision-making, leaving less to chance and more to choice.

Request a symbolic fee instead of working without a fee. Many architects request a symbolic fee rather than working entirely without compensation. Quoting a figure in the realm of £2,000 to £10,000 serves as an effective means of testing if a particular client has serious intentions and whether they value architectural work fairly.

Reduce the scope of work for unpaid services. Strategically reduce the scope of the deliverables for unpaid service by providing fast hand sketches, or volume studies, without defining details. Entice a client's imagination with a few strategic images and figures to acquire a full commission.

Negotiate follow-up conditions. Accept the unpaid work only on the condition that the client retains your architectural services should the project continue. A simple letter endorsed by the client in this case is sufficient.

Negotiate a next project. Enquire whether the client will commission your services for other projects, should this one not be successful. Be wary of setting a precedent with a potentially large client of initially working without a fee. Consider strategically whether it is worthwhile to initially work without a fee.

Negotiate a bonus. Commercial project developers, in particular, appreciate it if you take a risk by making an unpaid sketch. By negotiating a success fee or bonus you can receive payment if the project continues.

Emphasise your flexibility. Ensure that your client understands that free work is an exception. It is important that the client realises that your work, in this particular case, is a gift.

Solicit your own work by approaching the right parties with your ideas. With unsolicited proposal work (unpaid) it is possible to generate your own commission. If you identify a vacant site with potential, you might sketch a concept for its revitalisation and approach a developer. This kind of active acquisition works for some architects. However, as in all things, balance is key. How much time is it wise to invest and what happens if this does not have the desired outcome?

CHAPTER 2
WE CAN DO BETTER

The pursuit of a larger, humane ideal is often the inspiration for architects' work and practice. They create spaces for people, so design often aims to enhance quality of life, community benefits and user experience. This implies that architects are socially concerned and, further, that we can reasonably assume they treat their workforce with the same deference they do the future occupants of their buildings. Sadly, this is not always the case. The architectural profession is one of the lowest-paid professions requiring a university education and the combination of low wages and frequent overwork exacerbates discontent, cutting short many promising careers.

In fairness, this is a condition that is often cemented in the early days of a practice. Founders fully dedicate themselves to establishing the firm, and experience considerable success as a result. Once they hire their first employees, excessive work defines their company culture. This serf-like attitude is adopted by both owners and employees. Harsh competition justifies evening and weekend work, taking its toll on personal life.[1] As a business model, this lowers costs and makes it possible for young architecture practices to compete, offering a price comparable to that of a developing country, where working 100 hours and being paid for 40 is typical. This ruinous working culture ideally subsides once the practice becomes more settled; however, in many practices these old habits die hard.

There is a certain glamour in this lifestyle, and many young architects see this sacrifice as a rite of passage. The cycle perpetuates when they establish their own practices with this ethos. There are countless reports online of the abuse that takes place in starchitects' offices, but this is just as common in small practices. Across the board, it is morally wrong to base a business model on the excessive work of poorly paid employees. Increasingly, the industry has been taken to task for the flaws of this parasitic model. In 2019, the naming and shaming of architects who do not pay their interns resulted in a public outcry, to the detriment of several high-profile architecture practices' reputations.[2]

It is clear that architecture is not an easy business to succeed in, but at the same time, reliance on the unpaid work of employees as a business model is not a sound solution. There is a demonstrated link between poor business practice and exploitation; if the fee negotiated with a client for work to be done falls short of professional standards for time and effort required, the burden often falls on staff in excessive overtime.

The almost vocational dedication to what is commercial work can cause strains in an architect's personal life. Recall the scene from the film *The Devil Wears Prada* (2006) where Andy tries in vain to explain to her friends why she cannot go out with them, and they wonder what the big fuss is about some dresses. This happens in architecture. Even if the architect you work for is world famous, this fame is only relevant in your bubble and your friends and family might wonder why you dedicate so much hard work to 'just a building'. In this case, the indentured architect's struggle is two-fold: labour is hard and offers poor compensation, and personal life suffers as you endlessly fall short of expectations, repeatedly having to apologise, explain and defend the lifestyle.

PRACTICAL TIPS FOR MANAGING HARD-LABOUR CONDITIONS

Get paid. Easier said than done, but implement controls and sufficiently schedule deliverables to ensure that you receive payment for the full services you provide.

Plan ahead. Planning your work well will ensure success. Endlessly exploring options can be a wonderful means of innovating but fail fast, iterate rapidly and commit to efficiency.

Involve clients in decision-making. Avoid working in a black hole. Involve the client more frequently to expedite decisions and reduce unnecessary workflow.

Make communal decisions. Plan the overwork together with your employees. Be there and do the same hours as your employees, or more.

Enhance secondary benefits. If you cannot pay your employees for the full services they provide, seek out opportunities to make their lives easier, by offering other employment benefits. Maybe share some of the perks of your professional life with your employees – think about taking them to interesting meetings or site visits. It will be great for morale and motivation.

Be open. An open discussion and transparency between you and your employees is important. You can discuss future ambitions and agree that the current work style is a means to an end – an investment in a future without overwork.

Be grateful. Be aware that people work overtime voluntarily and that this is a gift of a precious resource. Be grateful and respectful of this.

Do better. Although you might have endured abuse yourself as a young architect, do not perpetuate this tradition.

CHAPTER 3
TO SPECIALISE OR NOT TO SPECIALISE?

In architectural education around the world, architecture students learn to be well-rounded design professionals. They learn to design anything from private residences to public buildings; from skyscrapers to airport terminals; they conduct academic research and typological studies. When released into the real world, they are quickly confronted with a tender system that favours firms with built experience, experience that recent graduates and young firms do not yet have. Regulations demand that architecture practices provide evidence of realised buildings of a similar typology, so they favour the large firm of practised architects. Only if an architect has built five town halls in the last five years does the (often) public client believe that town hall number six can be successfully executed.

This system is problematic because it stifles innovation and articulates the lack of connection between academia and the practice of architecture. With a broad experience in architecture practices accumulated over the last 21 years, it is my belief that in practice, academia rightfully educates future architects as *homo universalis*, with a well-rounded exposure to designing different building typologies. Acquiring this dexterity is important because it allows architects to think beyond a single typology. It forces students to be flexible and – as architects are often the central coordinating point in complex projects – it helps them manage diverse stakeholders, from contractors to public participation professionals.

When MVRDV was founded, its first project was a 10,000m^2 office building for a Dutch public broadcasting corporation (Figure 3.1). The three young founding partners had some experience working in other practices, but did not yet know how to technically realise a building. They devised a project that would become famous through its innovative concept; they realised it by gathering experts around them who knew how to make a building. Of course, they made mistakes that another more experienced practice would not have made: acoustics were problematic, for example. After having addressed the error by applying acoustic materials, the building was well received and it kick-started a company that now has more than 250 employees. This was the Netherlands of the 1990s. In the context of today's (generally highly relevant) EU tender regulations, this kind of instant start-up based on talent is simply not possible.

Figure 3.1 *Villa VPRO, Hilversum, the Netherlands, MVRDV, 1997 – the first realised project by the then young architects Winy Maas, Jacob van Rijs and Nathalie de Vries. Today it is increasingly difficult for young architects to start a practice with a sizable project.*

In the eyes of many investment parties or public clients, projects are too complex or risky to be left to inexperienced architects. The stakes are too high. Even experienced firms have difficulty acquiring projects if they do not have the right references. For example, despite 27 years of experience, MVRDV does not have sufficient references to win a tender for a school in the Netherlands. However, MVRDV won a school commission in Denmark due to a different interpretation of EU tender rules. Around the world, a relatively small number of select architecture practices are responsible for airport design. The same applies in many countries for stations, hospitals, prisons and so on. These typological monopolies can result in prominent public buildings that are rather repetitive and lack innovation.

Thankfully, there are some wonderful exceptions. The Berlin Tegel project (1974) remains a highly appreciated and alternative airport design. This was the seminal work of the very young architects Meinhard von Gerkan, Volkwin Marg and Klaus Nickels, who did not have a single built structure in their portfolio when they won the commission. In 2019, Jeanne Gang won the design for a large terminal at Chicago O'Hare. Although Studio Gang is long established, the firm does not have another airport in their portfolio. Sadly, these are exceptions to the general rule.

Figure 3.2 *Tegel Airport, Berlin, GMP Architects, 1974. Berlin Tegel Airport is a highly acclaimed work by the then young architects Meinhard von Gerkan, Volkwin Marg (pictured, on the right) and Klaus Nickels.*

If we consider specialisation from a positive perspective, it offers the opportunity for architects to become experts in a particular building typology. These firms easily win public tenders because they have the right references. For the public client, this offers security and an efficient workflow. Mitigating risk is a strong directive in many tender procedures and expert architects use this to their advantage.

Business wise, specialisation can be extremely profitable. However, it presents some inherent risks. Consider what might happen if the market for your specialism collapses. What if all train stations are built and renovated and for the next 10 years nothing happens? Does the niche architect go bankrupt? During the 2008–2014 economic crisis, architecture practices with mainly public clients experienced the crisis later than those with a more diverse portfolio. This was because public projects often carried on despite the difficult economic situation. However, two or three years into the crisis, the public work in many European countries came to a halt. Specialised practices either had time to foresee the coming change and adapt by diversifying their portfolio, or they were too comfortable, took little action and were hit hard. Firms that had diversified had found alternative means of managing the economic downturn.

Having a clear vision of your firm's portfolio and specialisation range is one means of mitigating risk and reducing dependence on any specific client or building typology. An architect who decides to specialise in libraries, for example, has a clear vision of the kind of work they wish to engage in. A set specialism is a solid means of focusing all acquisition work. It is a risk, however, should the market dry up.

PRACTICAL TIPS REGARDING SPECIALISATION

- **Select more than one specialism.** If specialisation is the right choice for your practice because you are, for example, interested in private residences or office buildings, consider the volatility of the market in which you are operating. Strategically select a small number of specialisations. For example, Henning Larsen Architects, based in Denmark, focus on four strong points: cultural landmarks, educational facilities, urban plans and offices.
- **Assemble a complementary team or consortium.** Some architects have been successful in applying for tenders in teams or in joint ventures with other practices with the right references. When shaping such a team, it should be clear what each partner will obtain from the arrangement. For example, a new small local firm in combination with a large experienced practice can be highly attractive to local councils or clients who want to encourage young local entrepreneurs. In this case, the collaboration strategy is interesting for the large experienced practice, who will acquire local connections, presence and knowledge. This translates into a higher chance of success. If you are a fledgling architecture practice, why not be bold and approach the behemoths with your insight and opportunity to collaborate?

Adapt your presentation and proposal to address the unique qualities of the tender. Instead of duplicating the documents you put together for your last tender, adapt your presentation, adding diagrams or hand sketches. Guide the eye of the potential client towards your experience: imagine you apply for an office building but you have no reference except for a library that has a restaurant, offices and educational spaces. You can still use the reference but you should highlight the office space in the building. For small projects, this approach can also apply: think about a home with a large home-working space. Perhaps you can use it as a reference for a small office project.

Review the case studies of companies interviewed for this book. They have each determined a means of uniquely managing specialisation. Consider your specialisation, describe it in writing as an exercise in clarification and discuss it with someone when in doubt.

Petition local authorities to adjust their tender procedures. Are you frustrated by not being able to design a small public building because as a young architect you do not yet have sufficient references? Protest. Local authorities can organise their tender procedures differently. And you need not do this alone. Approach architectural peers and other practices, or perhaps even the press, to join you in your petition. The RIBA and other national architectural institutes and organisations can also provide support. This may not impact the project you would like to influence, but in the long term it may change procedures to support less experienced practices. Frequent and consistent petitions against tendering rules are the most effective means of changing the game.

CHAPTER 4
MARKETING: A DIRTY WORD IN ARCHITECTURAL CIRCLES

Well done. You've got your hands on a book about selling architecture. Here's a bit of hard truth for you: architecture practices are capitalist entities that are sustained by earning money and making profit. Nevertheless, words like 'sales' or 'commercial' are not especially popular among architects. Large practices have sales departments, but even they rarely call themselves by their real name. Euphemisms such as 'business development', 'communication and strategy' or even 'the Kitchen', as is the case with Herzog & de Meuron, conceal their actual purpose, which is to drive sales.

Many architects wish to maintain an intellectual purity, in spite of the fact that in today's society even museums have highly successful and effective sales or acquisition teams. Behind the semantics is a certain hesitation towards the commercial or business side of the practice, if not outright disdain. This is not a useful perspective to maintain because the success of each acquisition defines the future of your practice. Therefore, it is important that you actively pursue acquisitions in a way that suits you and does not violate your standards of good taste. Getting good at it is key to the success of your practice.

There are brands that are incredibly successful when it comes to capturing architects' attention. Take, for example, the popularity that Martin Margiela's four white dots have enjoyed with architects, or Comme des Garçons' heart with eyes, Freitag bags, recognisable Camper shoes, minimalist COS clothing and USM furniture. Architects are a target audience like any other. An entire industry stands to profit significantly from targeting architects. Oddly enough, the target audience for the marketing of construction materials (tiles, glass, piping, etc.) is younger, and perhaps even more impressionable, architects.[1]

If you are sceptical of marketing, you are not alone. However, when you take time to master sales, public relations and acquisitions, you can create significant impact for your business. This might be the key to acquiring the projects that you dream of, and generating decent salaries for your staff. Don't be afraid – dare to become good in marketing, in a way that best suits your practice.

CHAPTER 5
MISSION AND VISION

For a small architecture practice, mission and vision statements might be a tediously commercial venture. However, the more definition these statements have, and the more you and your staff agree on them, the more practical they become when trying to reach your goals. For example, often when I visit other architecture offices, the principal explains clearly what the practice does and stands for. Yet when I then encounter a long-serving staff member, and I ask them what their practice does, the answers vary. It is important that all staff know what the essence is, your raison d'être.

Writing your mission and vision statements is not all you must do to clarify your raison d'être. You should also explain them to your staff and your clients, and you could try to transform them into an elevator pitch. An elevator pitch is a 30-second summary of what you do and stand for – short enough for an elevator ride. With this, you and your staff can tell anyone very clearly what your practice does, and what drives your business.

In essence, the mission statement concerns what you are doing today, whereas the vision statement is about the future and your goal. In short, the mission (how) leads to the vision (why).

However you want to go about writing your mission and vision statements is up to you. Perhaps your mission and vision are so simple and clear that you can do it by yourself. That said, as a group process within a company, the experience can be valuable for generating and consolidating these ideas.

For the mission statement, you would answer the following questions:
- What do we do?
- How do we do it?
- Who do we do it for?

And for the vision statement, you could answer these questions:
- What do we bring to the world, to the discipline or to our clients?
- What do we change?
- What are our hopes and dreams?

First construct the statements in short and clear sentences. You can begin with a longer text and then condense this to a one-liner. This is a great exercise in evaluating the essence of your ambition. At MVRDV, it took us some time to condense our statement because we had trouble letting go of adverbs in the original vision statement.

It is useful to think about your target audience, the portfolio you desire, the services you want to provide and your unique selling points – what defines you and separates you from others? The vision statement is about your ambitions, so don't be shy in mentioning them, even if it is not possible to realise them immediately. It is important to have a long-term outlook. What is the goal you are pursuing?

Keeping the vision and mission open is not a bad thing, so don't limit yourself. If you want to change it after a while, don't be afraid to make adjustments. The mission and vision statements serve you and the further development of your company, so change them whenever you feel like it, or whenever you must change course.

PRACTICAL TIPS REGARDING MISSION AND VISION

Communicate clearly. Keep your statements short and clear so that people can remember them.

Be realistic. Lofty ambitions are great, but your small company with two people at start-up is not going to be able to solve world hunger. Orientate your statement using words such as 'contributing to …' rather than 'solving…'. You can always adjust later.

Ask your staff for input. Ask your staff what they think, and whether they can support the statements you make. This can lead to incredibly fruitful conversations about the reason for your work.

Draft an elevator pitch. Turn your statements into an elevator pitch and practise this with your staff so they can reproduce it in chance encounters.

Publish and present your statements. If you have mission and vision statements that you want other people to adopt, use them in public and talk about them. For example, if you tell people that you are dedicated to sustainable architecture, a potential client who hears this, and feels the same, might just want to work with you.

Assess. Have regular sessions (every one to three years) to check if you are still in agreement with your initial mission and vision. If not, adapt.

EXAMPLES OF MISSION AND VISION STATEMENTS

Company: Tesla
Mission: To accelerate the world's transition to sustainable energy.
Vision: To create the most compelling car company of the 21st century by driving the world's transition to electric vehicles.

Company: TED
Mission: Spread ideas.
Vision: We believe passionately in the power of ideas to change attitudes, lives and, ultimately, the world.

Company: Ferrari
Mission: We build cars, symbols of Italian excellence the world over, and we do so to win on both road and track. Unique creations that fuel the Prancing Horse legend and generate a 'World of Dreams and Emotions.'
Vision: Ferrari, Italian Excellence that makes the world dream.

Company: IKEA
Mission: Offer a wide range of well-designed, functional home furnishing products at prices so low that as many people as possible will be able to afford them.
Vision: To create a better everyday life for the many people.

CHAPTER 6
BRANDING AND COMPANY CULTURE

'Corporate identity' might make some architects feel nauseous, but for many – especially those who are great designers – it comes naturally (even though they might not want to call it 'branding' or 'corporate identity'). From the moment you design your first business card, you make a choice that ignites your branding. OMA's decision to use a sober typeface like Arial is a clear choice for this modernist practice's logo, while the postmodern architecture practice RAMSA finds a Times New Roman style more appealing.

For many years, architectural identities adopted minimalist approaches. I remember when I invited a Dutch graphic designer to design a corporate identity, and they refused, claiming: 'We will never again work for architects: it starts with lots of ideas, and then it changes into a messy process with half the practice, and the result is a black-and-white minimalist identity.' More often now, I see practices daring to use colour, and employ different fonts (Figure 6.1) in their corporate identity in order to differentiate themselves. However, this corporate identity must be genuine, and suitably aligned with your architectural style and philosophy. It is part of, not divorced from, your identity.

Most importantly, it should enhance the aura of your work while being practical. Fonts that cannot be read easily (many decision-makers are at the age where they need the assistance of reading glasses) or fonts that warp

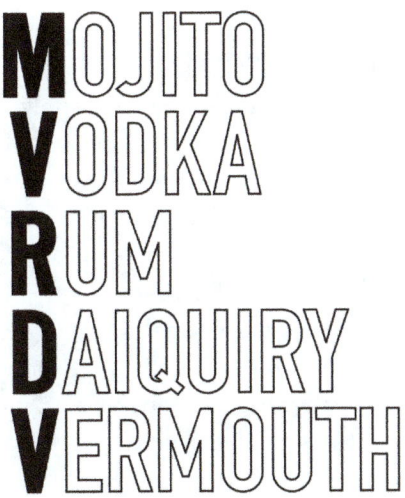

Figure 6.1 *An alternative meaning of MVRDV, as used for parties, and developed by an advertising agency that wanted to express the fun side of the practice.*

the moment you open a PowerPoint presentation on another computer are simply not practical.

To this end, address your corporate identity from a holistic perspective. Touch all the graphic products of your practice with the same brush, and consider their physical appearance as a total package. Liverpool architects shedkm (see Case Study 1) create modernist architecture, and hanging in their office is an oversized image of Le Corbusier. This is all part of their product, brand and philosophy. Studio MUTT's Liverpool office echoes the yellow hue used on their website, so branding and corporate identity permeate all facets of the practice's public presentation (see Case Study 3).

An even more holistic approach achieves cohesion in your architectural design style, your branding, mission, vision and company culture. If your practice is devoted to public participation projects, it would make sense to have a strong company culture that similarly engages employee participation. If your company creates slick, commercial architecture, it would be wise to have frequent self-development classes to further enhance these qualities in your company culture. Just make sure that what you do is authentic and suitable for your architectural philosophy, within which you design (read: preach).

There is an element of aspiration necessary in order to become the practice you want to be in the future. Base your company branding on the ambitions you have for the future.

PRACTICAL TIPS REGARDING BRANDING AND COMPANY CULTURE

- **Be authentic.** A cohesion of branding and company culture is evident only if the branding is authentic.
- **Articulate your identity.** Identity refers to you and your values. Ensure that your values are authentic, and that these are in line with your architecture.
- **Hire a graphic designer.** Graphic design is a profession for which individuals undergo significant training. Having a graphic designer evaluate your graphic corporate identity is worthwhile, even if you think you know better. You will (and you should) enter into a challenging discussion with your graphic designer, but the sparring is worth the trouble, as your identity will become more defined.

Use the identity you have created in all you do. Once you have taken time to develop the identity, use it. Architects are often too creative to always use the same book design template. However, from a branding perspective, it is valuable if your website, business card, office and staff (company culture) all resonate.

Develop your company culture. Finding the right match is an important challenge. A commercial practice is a different place than a practice devoted to cultural or social architecture. What you offer your staff communicates this difference. For some practices, it can be a slick office with a company-car scheme and suits. This will attract a certain kind of employee. Other offices will offer a vegan lunch, massages and mindfulness training. Consider the type of individuals you want to gather in support of your goals and make sure they understand your values.

Agree on an appropriate dress code. Discuss the kind of clothing that matches your firm's philosophy and – this quickly becomes personal – make a decision together, if this gets challenging. This might sound extremely corporate, until you meet a big new client, and your project leader appears in jeans and trainers.

CHAPTER 7
'IF I WAS DOWN TO MY LAST DOLLAR, I WOULD SPEND IT ON PR'

According to legend in the public relations world, Bill Gates is responsible for this powerful piece of advice. Whether or not this is true, it isn't surprising that his name is linked to this quote, as he has personally experienced the effects of good PR. This advice rings true across industries. The sports brand behemoth Nike spent a whopping $3.75 billion in 2019 on PR and marketing alone.[1] While IT and sports moguls embrace PR's value, in the typical architecture practice it can be a dirty word. Its value and influence are often belittled. How many times have I heard an architect mutter dismissively, 'It's a PR story' if they think that PR has manipulated public perception?

Public relations (PR) is the long-term structuring of a practice's reputation, as opposed to business development (BD), which is the short-term acquisition of projects, via tenders or direct client contact. In this sense, PR is a long-term investment in reputation development, often with no small measure of uncertainty as to where the road is leading. For example, sending out a press release can be a bit of a gamble, whereas a meeting with a potential client is a much more specific, concerted effort. PR and BD are both elements of marketing which work together. PR builds the reputation and BD yields the projects. Many small architecture practices manage just one of the two, focusing entirely on PR or on BD, yet they are most effective in combination. Larger practices typically have an integrated approach to marketing.

How architecture practices choose to build their reputation through PR activity is their prerogative, but it is most effective if approached authentically. Authentic, in this sense, means that it best suits the company and the architects tasked with managing PR. While conducting research for this book, I visited Oriel Chambers in Liverpool. This was the world's first building to feature a metal-framed glass curtain wall. Designed by architect Peter Ellis and built in 1864, the imposing building is the home of several architecture practices. Along a nondescript corridor on the third floor, I find two practices with very different approaches to PR. Both are excellent, but could not be more different.

Established in 2011, MgMaStudio (see Case Study 2) describe their approach to PR as personal. They tell me that in Liverpool, all PR is accomplished face-to-face. In the Liverpool business climate, PR means networking.

For new kids on the block, meeting the potential clients – often from an older, established generation – is no easy task. To tackle this, they invented 'Prosecco Friday' and invited everyone to share a bottle of bubbles. For a number of years, this PR worked well for the practice, but not so much for their livers. As the practice grew, they changed tack to become patrons of the Liverpool Philharmonic, so they could meet potential clients in person, at performances. Today, MgMaStudio have a wonderful portfolio, including impressive transformation projects just opposite Oriel Chambers.

Further down the corridor, I had the pleasure of speaking to Studio MUTT, a young practice (see Case Study 3). Studio MUTT got their start with a small self-financed structure in the Lake District: the Ordnance Pavilion. This colourful, Memphis-style object in the imposing landscape became a real Instagram sensation, and drove the practice to fame in short order. Studio MUTT now have commissions with commercial and public clients, such as the British Council, Sir John Soane's Museum and a hotel opposite the Three Graces.

These are neighbouring practices with completely different approaches to PR. One invests in networking, and the other in the power of new media. Both have found a sweet spot and success as a result. These approaches work because they suit their individual personalities.

Despite the fact that in many architecture offices PR has a lower status than the more noble creative process of architecture, there is a longstanding tradition of architects being effective through PR. Early starchitects such as Marcel Breuer, Le Corbusier and Mies van der Rohe were masters of using mass media to grow their business and reputation. A wonderful contemplation on the subject is the article 'Mies Not' by Beatriz Colomina,[2] which describes just how well conceived and meticulously designed and shaped Mies van der Rohe's public image was. Marcel Breuer's photo opportunities with Jacqueline Kennedy, Mies' staged portraits and Le Corbusier's legendary persona are all examples of their effective PR activities. Any architects who own a good-taste-oozing Barcelona Chair but are at the same time sceptical of PR would be well advised to reflect on why they have this particular chair, and how it became so famous. It is no coincidence, but a planned and premeditated Miesian PR strategy, which resulted in his portrayal as subtle and sophisticated.

In the sections that follow, I explain PR's endless potential. My intention is to inspire and inform, but it is your decision as to how this should translate to your firm's particular situation and available talent. What would be effective and authentic for your practice?

7.1 WRITING A MARKETING STRATEGY

Perhaps you are convinced that marketing is important. So, how do you get started? Write a marketing strategy so that there is a road map in place. This is part of a comprehensive business plan for your company, and therefore the marketing plan is the 'How to' of your business plan.

You know your business and what drives it, so making a marketing strategy begins with you. It's not difficult. Begin by writing down what you want to achieve and then envision the steps that will help you achieve these goals. Keep it simple and general to start. Later, you can make it more precise and add complexity.

This is a step-by-step approach to creating a marketing plan (with examples in brackets). Begin by identifying and describing:
- your offering (for example, single family homes)
- your unique selling point (wooden buildings that produce energy)
- what you want to accomplish in one year (focus on family homes for now)
- what you want to achieve in five years (venture into collective housing)
- who your clients are (affluent families with a green heart, in Cumbria)
- how you can reach these clients (meeting them in places that they frequent, advertising, [social] media, etc.)
- an action plan, including timeline and budget (by first meeting all possible available contacts, by starting a social media campaign or by going to a home builders' fair)
- the kind of projects you want to achieve in the longer term and the kind of opportunities you should take advantage of (for example, to tender four times a year for collective housing projects, to find a partner who would collaborate with you on collective housing, etc.).

This might sound excessively simple, but this exercise is useful for start-ups as much as for a large practice. By recording these goals and steps to achievement in a simple structured text, we liberate the plan from complexity at the outset. This makes it easier to focus on what's important.

THE BUSINESS MODEL CANVAS

For many entrepreneurs – those starting out or long established – the Business Model Canvas (BMC) is a useful means of creating a marketing plan and a business plan (Figure 7.1.1). The fact that the BMC is visual makes it a nice tool for architects, and it directs your thinking along very clear lines. You start by defining your key activities, key resources and then your partner network. You then think about what you offer, your value proposition, and you assess customer segments, channels and customer relationships. All of this is based on your cost structure and revenue stream. The BMC is incredibly easy to use and its content easy to find. Google the term, buy the book or hire consultants to help you write your own business model, including a marketing plan.

JUST DO IT!

This is perhaps the most important advice I can share with an ambitious practice. If you do no PR, there is little chance you will succeed. Being an architect with a practice also means that you are an entrepreneur. At a certain point, you need to take action to acquire new projects. Over the years, I have met many young architects who toyed with the idea of active acquisition and PR but were hesitant to begin. They saw this as a daunting task, and were terrified of doing the wrong thing. Rest assured, you will

The Business Model Canvas

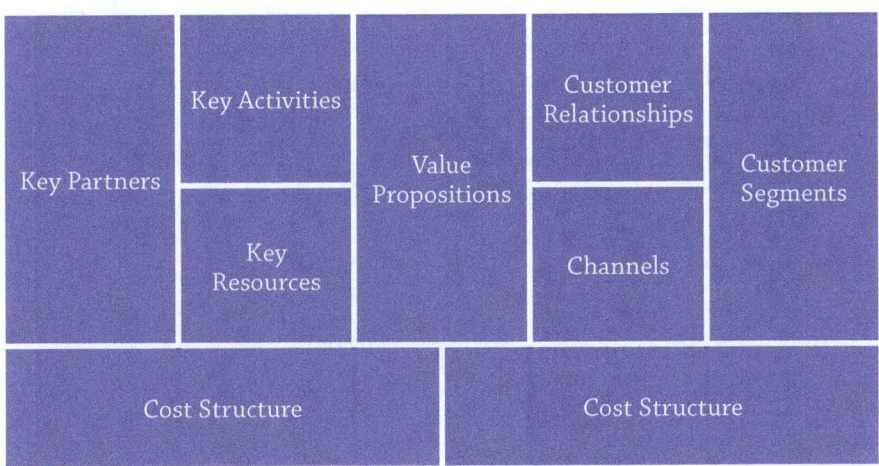

Figure 7.1.1 *The Business Model Canvas, by Strategizer, is an incredibly useful tool to create a business plan and marketing strategy.*

make mistakes. You will have some unsuccessful acquisitions, but if you invest attention and time, you will experience success as well. Remember, when you have a clear vision, you will know best which projects you'd like to design and build. You can inspire people and find clients that will want the same. Look how quickly the young Bjarke Ingels became successful after he started PLOT. At the same time, consider how visionaries like Zaha Hadid and Jan Kaplický had to struggle for decades because they had such an avant-garde approach to architecture. It took many years to convince clients of the value of their vision. Wherever you are on this scale, it is helpful to make a plan, contemplate how marketing can help you mobilise that plan and think about how to acquire new projects. Then, get to work. If you fail, regroup and refine your strategy.

PRACTICAL TIPS FOR WRITING AN EFFECTIVE MARKETING STRATEGY

Define your USP. It's terrible marketing slang but unavoidable: what is your unique selling point? Be aware of your strength, and what makes you stand out from all the other architects around.

Craft a business plan. Writing a business plan will help you order your thoughts. Even though it might never materialise exactly in the way you have written it down, it clears your thoughts, gives direction and allows you to focus. The business plan is not a bible; you can rewrite it whenever you think it needs adaption. Part of the business plan is the marketing plan.

Test ideas. Share your business plans and ideas with people you trust to make them that much more legible. Get advice wherever you can, and should you have staff, make sure they know about your goals and the actions you will take to achieve them. This way, they can contribute in their best way. This is important. The Seattle Public Library is, in my opinion, one of OMA's most important projects and it began because the mother of one of OMA's architects told her son that the project was up for tender. He knew that OMA was interested in this kind of project. Do your staff know what you want to achieve?

Just do it! Again, this is a very important part of the task. Don't spend too much time in theory, get down to the practical activity of trying to acquire projects. Are you a social character? Get out there and network. Are you introverted? Craft a social media campaign or participate in a few tender procedures. Either approach will work, but you must take action.

CHAPTER 8
THE OFFICE IS YOUR BUSINESS CARD

For many architects, a very simple yet effective form of PR is designing your office in the spirit and philosophy of your practice. This space represents your work, and it is a pragmatic means of demonstrating to guests, many of whom will be potential clients, that the work your studio delivers is both pleasant and inspiring.

MVRDV has experienced a learning curve in this respect. Twice the practice has moved into new industrial spaces and designed practical but inspiring offices. However, after a few years, spaces showed traces of wear and tear and began to look a little tired. Dust on blue foam models, black marks of shoes on the floor and quick-fix repairs communicated a creative but careless look and feel.

When MVRDV moved into a series of factory buildings, we designed another wonderful series of spaces with monochrome meeting rooms (Figure 8.1). It also includes a dedicated public zone, as well as tranquil working spaces. This separation allows architects to focus on their work, but also for the office to receive many client guests, as well as architecture-tourists. Our open-door policy forms a key pillar in the practice's PR policy.

Figure 8.1 *The MVRDV House, Rotterdam, MVRDV, 2016. The studio was designed to be a suitable representation of the practice's approach to architecture, featuring monochrome meeting rooms and a public area for visitors.*

Although the space was highly functional and attractive, after this move it took a mere three months before it began to show the first signs of wear and tear, or careless inconsistencies, with grey lecterns appearing in orange rooms. It was time for action. I determined that if we can't treat our own office with care and love, we can't ask our clients to respect our creations. So we rebranded our concierge our 'building curator' and gave him strict instructions to treat the office like a piece of art. This meant that all repairs were carried out swiftly, and that everything added to the interior was in the spirit of MVRDV, from wall decorations to woefully necessary reminders to flush toilets. All this was to demonstrate to our clients that we respect architecture and know how to make a space feel positive and fun. It is no doubt a struggle to maintain an office that houses 250 people, even though its own creators are in its workforce.

If we briefly return to the Oriel Chambers in Liverpool, home to MgMaStudio and Studio MUTT (see Chapter 7 and Case Studies 2 and 3), we see that both practices have created their own fitting interiors into the more generic interiors of the building. When sitting in Studio MUTT's 4m x 4m room, a yellow table and some art pieces by Studio Job communicate the feeling of the architectural work of this young firm, while MgMaStudio created a sober and tasteful interior much in line with their architecture. Both interiors enable clients to be received in spaces that communicate the personality of the firm. A well-designed office that reflects your thinking does not need to be highly expensive.

Needless to say, a quality cup of coffee or tea, a healthy snack, good bathroom towels and well-maintained dishware are important to complete your image and express a professional standard. Make no mistake, for many clients your office fundamentally represents your attitude towards architecture. Poor presentation or mistakes in your interior reflect badly on you and your work. Why? You are an architect, and creating successful spaces must be your core offer. For Feilden Fowles (see Case Study 6), this was such an important issue that they moved into a temporary structure in London designed according to circular-economy principles. They work in it and adhere to their beliefs and philosophy, organising countless events and using the structure to their advantage.

PRACTICAL TIPS FOR CREATING THE RIGHT KIND OF OFFICE

Reflect your work. Ask yourself whether your office reflects your work and your work philosophy. For example, if you are a practice that creates 'green' architecture, you need to live it and not have anything in the practice that contradicts this philosophy, such as plastic cups.

Use the resources you have available; any budget works. Creating a suitable interior does not require a significant investment. It is possible to reach this even with second-hand or IKEA furniture, if used in a convincing way.

Be a good host. This might be self-evident, but it's important to mention that you should aspire to be a good host, and think about the physical route your potential client will take: from the first impression, to the wardrobe, to the meeting room, as well as the food and drinks you present, the cups and plates, and the bathroom.

Explain yourself. If the office is not up to standard, don't be afraid to address this and even apologise. If the office is your pride and joy, explain why it is. Give your clients a tour imbued with your thinking related to the office you created.

Team spirit. Make sure that your employees understand and share the values you want to show in your office. From the receptionist to the project leaders, everybody should understand and embrace the office culture.

CHAPTER 9
YOUR WEBSITE: YOUR ONLINE SHOP WINDOW

Just as fundamental to your business as a physical office, your firm's website is a representation of your practice, your work and your philosophy. In this way, the website is comparable to a shop window. It illustrates what you have on offer.

First, your website is a powerful communication tool. As always in communication, it is important to begin by asking yourself a few questions. Who do you want to engage? What do you want to tell your online visitors? What do they want? Before building your website, ensure that you have a clear idea of who your audience is and what you want to achieve when they visit your site.

Your website has two main functions:
- to enhance and expand your reputation (PR)
- to help sell your product (BD).

You achieve the first goal by ensuring that your website reflects the look, feel and graphic style of your work. This can be a daunting task. How do you translate an innovation-based philosophy into a website? Does this mean that the website needs to be innovative too? How do you suggest through a website that you are a sustainable practice? Do you have to compensate for the electricity the website uses? Is it enough to have great texts that explain this or imagery that features solar cells? For many practices, the most workable solution is translating the corporate identity into the graphic style of their website.

Your potential clients, especially commercial clients, are often less interested in your cool factor and more interested in practical information. They want to be able to navigate to your project data quickly. A typical project developer's website search will relate to the project they want to execute with you, so they will assess whether you have worked in the same location, with the same scale, typology and complexity. For this kind of search, it is important that your site is easy to navigate and that you provide clear, fact-based information (date, location, surface, budget and function).

Balancing between the cool factor and rational information is at times a contradictory exercise and this can make architects' websites rather complex. The more projects you have, the better and more user-friendly your filter function should be. This allows for easy navigation. It will help your clients find the reference projects you want them to see.

Nevertheless, it is often difficult to strike a balance between the contradictory interests of different users. You have students who want to be inspired, architectural peers who want information and clients who want data. There are, of course, practices that enjoy the privilege of being at the very top of the food chain and can opt out of serving multiple user groups. Herzog & de Meuron and Zaha Hadid Architects, for example, have opted for more esoteric websites.[1] These are difficult to navigate because they sacrifice user-friendliness in favour of an innovative aesthetic appeal. This is likely a clear choice.

I have had the opportunity to build quite a few architects' websites and have often experienced that architects value design over user-friendliness. As an architect who is also an entrepreneur, you might want to ask friends and family if they enjoy visiting a website with eccentric functions such as pop-up windows. If you don't like them yourself, avoid them. Your clients will most likely experience the same challenges you do.

Instead of having lengthy discussions about style with your web designer, ask for their advice on functionality. Probe with questions such as, 'Is it likely that visitors will use a Facebook share button?' Or perhaps, 'What is the ideal text length for user reading?' These are essential questions and comparable to asking whether a room in a house you design will be used. Pay careful attention to user-friendliness, and how well your content will score in search engines. This will help you achieve your goal. User appeal, as opposed to aesthetic appeal, is becoming more and more important. Many architects' websites now feature a project search function that produces thumbnail-based search results, visually comparable to Google image searches, but prettier. Your clients know how these function from their experience with Google so they quickly catch on to site navigation. You don't want an over-designed website with poor functionality that irritates, rather than helps, clients and visitors.

There is another significant benefit to having an effective website. I pushed my first website through at OMA with the argument that it would save hiring another PR person by instead providing the right information online. This is true for practices that are popular with students and the media.

The more useful your website is to students and the media (as in, the faster they can access the information they need), the fewer emails you will have to answer. Unanswered emails give people the impression that your office is too arrogant to take time to answer, which does little to enhance your reputation.

ANALYTIC TOOLS

Google Analytics is a free tool provided by Google that allows you to monitor how your clients are using your website. It is extremely useful for tracking visitor behaviour and can illustrate, for example, the number of visitors from Nottingham or Inverness in real time. If available, it also provides information about the users, such as age and gender, as well as which pages on the website they visit. With this information, you can evaluate how your website performs, as this relates to your business goals. More importantly, it gives information about your potential clients. At MVRDV, we observed that our main cohort of visitors was Italian architecture students. As much as we loved the fact that we had so many Italian fans, this information was powerful, as we were aware of the fact that we had to take action to make the site more interesting to potential clients and decision-makers. One decisive step we took at MVRDV was to build links to our website into news-based posts on LinkedIn, geared towards reaching clients. These posts perform as 'feeders' to encourage decision-makers to visit the website.

On a larger scale, media-monitoring software that, for example, Meltwater or Bloomberg provide can help you monitor your entire online presence and check how effective you are in reaching your target audience (for example, potential decision-makers in real estate). This kind of software also provides information on whether the online sentiment about your practice is positive or negative. Information is king, because it allows you to take strategic steps to adjust sails as necessary. If a certain project you published receives overwhelmingly negative responses, you might wish to consider how you published it. There may be another aspect of the project that you could highlight to receive a more positive response. Change the approach and then evaluate performance with your analytics software.

A word of warning: using Google Analytics means that you contribute to Google's data collection efforts. It's free to use, but you indirectly pay by giving them access to your company's online data, and you need to mention its use in the information you need to provide to visitors of your website regarding the Data Protection Act. The monitoring software that Bloomberg,

Meltwater and others provide is expensive, and geared towards practices of a certain size, which have a dedicated budget for this kind of knowledge.

PRACTICAL TIPS FOR YOUR WEBSITE

Reflect your values. Your website speaks for you and should therefore reflect your values and philosophy. This should be expressed in content rather than in an edgy website structure. User-friendliness is as important a parameter for the design as your wish for high aestheticism.

Make your website user-friendly. Your potential clients expect to find the right information quickly, so make sure that your website performs as an acquisition device. This implies a certain level of practicality.

Use your website as a tool. With Google Analytics, you can monitor the effect of your website through the behaviour of users. Let's say you've built a website and have invested £15,000. Google Analytics informs you that your site has few visitors or perhaps not the visitors you wanted. With this information in hand, you can adjust your strategy to ensure that you achieve, at the very least, a return on your initial investment, and thereafter make the website work for you.

Respect your web designer's expertise. Architects are from Mars and web designers are from Venus. However much you might dislike their personal taste and style, web designers are the expert in this realm. Use their expertise to create a user-friendly, effective website that combines your ideas and designs with smart web functionalities.

Do some market research. Evaluate how your competitors present themselves online and determine if you should respond to this by doing something completely different, or by simply adhering to the industry standard. This is up to you to decide. Your decision relates to your original definition of your unique selling point. Also helpful is gleaning inspiration from high-performing, user-friendly websites that are not, in fact, architecture-related but excel in design, functionality or innovation.

Install Google Alerts. It's a free service of Google that allows you to have an automated daily search for your practice's name, your name or your projects. The result is delivered by email.

Prioritise your contact page. The contact section of your website is often the most-visited part. Make it easy to find and clear, and try to add some great information about your practice. Also be sure to claim your business on Google and add all necessary information (if you google your business, there is an 'Own this business?' button which allows you to add data). In this way, the contact information shows up correctly on Google searches.

CHAPTER 10
YOUR WORK AMID A CHANGING MEDIA LANDSCAPE

The media landscape has experienced dramatic changes over the last 20 years and the architectural media has evolved in tandem. In the late 1990s, getting published in *The New York Times* was the pinnacle of PR achievement. In fact, the paper's architecture critic, the late Herbert Muschamp, could make or break careers. A testament to his influence is the legendary 5,000-word Guggenheim Bilbao article he penned that cemented Frank Gehry's superstar status.[1] Print journalists' positive and negative perspectives had the power to sway public perception.

The rise of the internet and digital media has decentralised the journalist's authority and given rise to a new media model: online architectural journals such as *Dezeen* and *ArchDaily*. In the early days, these online journals could publish before most firms' press releases. At that time, their influence became unprecedented. It still is today. A publication on *Dezeen* means that your work reaches a broad and dispersed global audience. At the same time, this has opened channels of criticism to non-professionals, whose only authority is their opinion. Online media has given everyone a platform to wield devastatingly scathing blows, with comments as pithy as 'lame' having the potential to reach thousands upon thousands of people, depending on your follower count. In a few short years, 'lame', by 'Anonymous', might have gained more clout than a sophisticated 5,000-word critique.

With each day that passes, the media landscape increases in complexity, with more platforms and variety than ever before. However, Google amasses almost all advertising dollars. This creates significant strife for traditional magazines whose livelihoods depend on selling ad space, resulting in many having closed their doors forever. The basis of this change is a dying readership: ask a millennial whether they have bought a magazine recently; they are used to free online media.

The relative velocity of online media, and the comparative shortfall of funds in traditional media, has shifted considerable responsibility to architecture practices themselves. Firms must now create the content that has previously been the responsibility of editorial offices. We must cover the costs of professional photographs and manage our media profile, performing a role that the media controlled 20 years ago. The UK's 86,000 PR staff now outnumber its 73,000 journalists.² This is still solid but be warned: in the rapidly developing Dutch media climate, the outlook is dire. For each Dutch journalist, there are eight PR representatives gunning for journalists' attention.³ The next step in this evolution is scripting.

How do architects feel the impact? To start with, it is now our responsibility to deliver all manner of high-quality, professional and instantly publishable media products, at no expense: texts, photographs, renders and drawings. We also now enjoy the opportunity and the responsibility to communicate directly with the general public via social media platforms. Historically, the press functioned as a filter. They decided what the public would see. Now, anyone with a social media account can have their 15 minutes of fame. It is both a situation of intense competition for the few remaining traditional media outlets, as well as an incredible liberation, as we now have the ability to interact directly with our public.

Within this new world of opportunity, it is nevertheless important to return to the basics in order to decide how to manage this responsibility. We have to ask fundamental questions: who is our audience? What do we want to achieve? Do we want fame, new clients or peer recognition? Are we looking for a PR effect (reputation) or a BD effect (acquisitions)? When we define the answers, we can start to think about who we aim to address and determine the most appropriate means of doing so. For the benefit of reaching our desired audience, do we stick to traditional print media or online media? Do we run social media campaigns or do we focus on business-to-business media in order to reach decision-makers? Most importantly: how do we get there?

In order to succeed in PR, we need to envision where we would like to be and where to invest focus. Imagine a practice interested in commercial architecture with an ambition to build a corporate headquarters. Our target audience would be CEOs or operations managers of large corporations. Next question: where do we find them? Look for them on LinkedIn perhaps, or other business-to-business oriented media, or perhaps specialist media platforms. The challenge here is that this specialist media may not want to publish architecture, so in the meantime it is important that we do not neglect other media. It is often said that 'there is no such thing as bad publicity', so if you don't get any traction with your focus group, you may want to run with whatever yields a response, while still using targeted media as much as possible.

The choice is incredible. From the do-it-yourself Instagram campaigns (like that of Studio MUTT, see Case Study 3) to hiring well-connected London architecture PR firm Bolton & Quinn, to gaining coverage in broadsheets such as the *Financial Times* or *The Times*, anything is possible. The next few subchapters will touch upon different approaches to reaching readers, while also expanding on the communications side of an architecture firm's products: its renders, drawings and collages.

The best way to measure your PR impact is by calculating the equivalent of advertisement value. For example, if you have a quarter-page article about your work published in *The Guardian*, you can measure its monetary value by checking the advertisement rate for a quarter-page ad in this section of the newspaper, then add 10–30% because it's not an ad but an article, which is worth more. Remember that social media views also have an advertisement value. Calculating advertisement value by hand is a lot of work, so you may want to consider analytical software such as that offered by Bloomberg or Meltwater.

10.1 PRINT MEDIA

Despite sweeping changes in media, print media is still very relevant, both in paper editions and in digital versions. Daily print publications or magazines like *The Economist* are the most prestigious places to publish your work. What's challenging is the fact that they seldom write about architecture. When they do, they are most interested in developments in innovation and featuring architecture that represents new societal trends, such as green building or community-based architecture. Most concerned with details and controversy, they are likely to write about massive delays in projects or spiralling costs. For examples of this, consider the media coverage surrounding the Elbphilharmonie concert hall in Hamburg (see Chapter 24) or the City of Arts and Sciences in Valencia.

One thing to keep in mind is that news media publications are rather serious and require information immediately, due to press deadlines. Many operate according to a code of conduct that stipulates that you cannot see and edit the article before publication. When working with them, I would always recommend requesting permission to read their article to correct misinformation. Sometimes inviting news media journalists to the opening of your building works well, particularly if you pay their travel. A half page in *The New York Times* real estate section alone can cost up to $21,000. Compared to this, the cost of a flight, hotel and meal for a journalist is a fantastic deal should your chosen publication accept such an invitation. Many will; some won't. Business media and specialist media are also effective because of their business readership (decision-makers), but they are difficult to secure.

There is a vast array of magazines to publish in. I recently walked into a bookshop in Germany where a 2.5m-wide display had more than 100 architecture-related titles. However, many of these titles dealt with escapism and identification. Magazines like these are happy to publish private homes of less than 500m^2, which invite readers to dream of minimalist villas in Belgium, Chelsea townhouses or quaint French manor houses. Publishing features on villas owned by affluent clients is easy because readers love to see how those of a certain means live. These highly curated magazines offer glimpses into this dream. Publishing urban planning or collective housing with 200 apartments is more challenging.

The unique challenge with magazines is that they often have long production times and demand exclusivity. This also means that you have to wait up to three months before you can share the press release and publish it online. You must decide if the long wait is worth it. How? Assess whether the magazine is so prestigious that publishing with it will enhance your reputation. You can do this by determining whether the magazine has a readership that includes decision-makers in your target group, or whether by virtue of publishing with such an esteemed magazine, you might expect that other media will follow suit and share your content.

If you cannot wait, it may be possible to negotiate with the magazine for partial exclusivity. For example, partial exclusivity might mean that images the magazine publishes in the feature will not appear in any other media prior to the publication date. With buildings in large cities, any kind of exclusivity is difficult. While you wait for the magazine's publishing clauses to expire, you might be unlucky when a hapless Instagrammer claims the first bit of buzz for your new building and then you lose control.

Print media receives a lot of great news from all kinds of writers. Sending a pitch can work, but the chances are lower if it's a cold request than, for example, if you know a journalist or you know someone who does. If you have no PR connections, you can hire a professional PR agency. They come with a price, but are often worth the expense, as they have journalist contacts and will push your project into the right kind of media.

LOCAL NEWS

Local media is a specialist platform. Many cities still have a decent local newspaper, in addition to rapidly produced newspapers distributed door-to-door at no cost, informing you of what's happening in your own neighbourhood. Neighbourhood organisations and their stakeholders have power and can seriously impede or stop your project altogether. Treat these journalists with the same respect you would give the architecture critic of *The New York Times*.

BRAND MAGAZINES

A magazine published by a brand may approach you to publish your work. How do you respond? The fundamental question applies: will it help you reach your target audience? For example, *Porsche Magazine* will likely reach affluent people, and many people in the real estate business read British Airways' *High Life* magazine. The challenge is to assess whether or not the brand is in line with your own identity. If you are an architect dedicated to sustainable building, you might not want your work to appear in a magazine published by a company criticised for their contribution to global warming. This is a decision for you to make.

PRACTICAL TIPS FOR DEALING WITH PRINT MEDIA

- **Respect the power of these publications.** They are still the most prestigious. Even though the print media is in decline, it can still be incredibly effective. I'd advise you to make an extra effort to get your article in a well-read print medium. If you're in doubt, run a Google search for the print run. This will tell you about the reach and readership of the publication.
- **Be intentional.** Connect with journalists who may have an interest in the kind of work you produce, or in the kind of innovation you are authoring. Try to imagine yourself in their position and evaluate whether your project suits their newspaper.

Don't be shy. Print media works with many freelance journalists who write for their newspaper. If you have an interesting project coming up, contact a journalist from a relevant publication. Many newspapers publish their journalists' email addresses and many journalists have either a personal website or some form of social media.

Invite journalists to openings and events. This sounds simple, but journalists receive so many invitations that they have difficulty attending them all. Don't despair. Continue to invite them and possibly offer to cover the expense of their trip. If you do, ensure that they travel in comfort: first-class train and business-class flights, if money stretches to it. This kind of invitation makes the decision easier for newspaper editors because it reduces costs. The journalist will be encouraged to make the trip, so they might fight that much harder to publish a feature on your building opening in the newspaper.

Use Twitter. Many journalists use Twitter to keep up with news. This is a quick way to keep them up to date.

Accept exclusivity requirements. If the audience reach is valuable to you, and the deal is one you can't refuse, accept the magazine's exclusivity period.

Make friends. If there is a good connection between you and the journalist (authenticity here is integral), become friends with them. Invite them for lunch or drinks from time to time and casually keep them up to date about your activities. Also endeavour to learn from them how media trends are developing and find out what is interesting to them and their publication. It is important to be relevant and friendly.

Be prepared for crises to take priority. Say you work on an article for a publication and a crisis hits. Accept that your article is going to have less priority. For example, on 9/11, media had only one story to investigate, while regular news took a back seat.

Don't be disappointed with poor results. If your effort doesn't result in more work, at least you tried. Failure is no shame, because the competition in this industry is fierce.

10.2 ONLINE MEDIA

Online media is not the digital version of its print counterpart. It is media that is exclusively online, or media that has both a print identity and an online identity. For example, *Domus*, the renowned Italian architecture magazine, publishes different online content than it publishes in its print form.

The sheer reach of online media makes publishing online valuable. Just as print publications require research into the audience and brand implications, so does online media. It is still important to consider relevance and your target audience, which is likely different for each platform and medium. Reflect on which media is relevant to the work you want to feature and the audience you want to reach. Significant characteristics of online media include immediacy of placement and unique performance and function. There is also the possibility of going viral, amplifying the reach of your content beyond what you thought possible. To make online editors' work easy, you should write content that can be placed with minimal changes necessary. Also ensure that the imagery and video content you provide can be used free of charge. Margins are tight for online media, and few online publications are willing to pay for image rights. Make sure you own the rights, to prevent any impediments, and that you always send material under the condition that your name is mentioned.

DEZEEN, ARCHDAILY AND OTHERS

If you are very ambitious and you have high-quality work suitable for the likes of *Dezeen, Designboom* or *ArchDaily*, you have it made. The unique strength of these publications is that they are open and available to a globally dispersed audience. You will often see that many copycat websites publish the same content immediately after these big players; this is how content can go viral. The risk in this is that you may have to weather nasty reactions from the public.

If these comments are based on incorrect assumptions, you may want to react to correct them. It is best to do this as openly and honestly as possible, and under your own name. Clarify any incorrect information briefly and politely. Stay calm, and never enter an extensive debate. If the negative reactions are a reflection of taste, or include vague dismissive comments such as 'horrible' or 'ugly', refrain from commenting at all. You won't be able to argue about taste. Just enjoy the fact that your work is provocative enough to incite the interest of critics. A Dutch proverb states that 'tall trees catch wind'. If you have created a project that causes conversation and criticism, endure both the fame and the criticism. This won't be easy, but try not to take flippant comments too seriously. Some people do this for sport, and more often than not they do so under the cloak of anonymity. This says something about their motives. It might be less about you and more about frustration in their own life, with their work, their boss or a hefty parking fine.

SELF-PUBLISHING

If it is challenging for you to publish on established digital media channels, you can try to publish independently on blogs or websites that offer a membership and allow you to upload content yourself. For example, *Archello*, *Designboom* or *World Architecture* might be effective. In your project features, it is important to include a link to your own website. If this function is available, tag your projects, so that they appear in dynamic searches.

One challenge with digital media is that it is not always clear who you should contact. It can be difficult to determine which editing house is responsible for the site, or who is in charge. It is not always necessary to have this information, but it might be important for you. Some digital websites (like some print media) are part of a political movement that you may not endorse. The site might not value objective news. In the past, I have seen our work on the website of a tabloid. This is conflicting. On one hand, it's great to have the exposure to their broad readership. On the other hand, I wonder if we damage our reputation through association with a tabloid with strong political inclinations. Although we work for clients on all sides of the political spectrum, an article on this very outspoken platform could be criticised by the opposition. Funnily enough, the tabloid never gave us the choice, as they published without our permission.

A great benefit to publishing online is the length of time articles are accessible. Sometimes they're online for years. Another benefit is the sheer volume of readers that your work is exposed to. A website with a strong online presence attracts countless visitors, and this greatly enhances exposure to your work. Also, their Google search rankings are strong, meaning that your work has an even more broad reach.

PRACTICAL TIPS ABOUT ONLINE MEDIA

Take rejections in your stride. *Dezeen* and *ArchDaily* receive so many requests for publication that you should not be disappointed by rejection. Continue to try.

Exercise caution in the comment section. My advice would be, only react if the comments indicate that the reader has made an incorrect assumption. Refrain entirely from long debates over taste. Some people will hate your building, no matter what you say or do.

Link the article to your website. Linking your website to the online article will enhance your website's ranking in search engines.

Share the article on your relevant social media platforms. Sharing the online article on your social media can serve as a great information tool for your followers. Generally speaking, readers place more trust in a third party's feature pieces than in features you publish on your website's press room. So, I suggest linking to third-party articles about your work on your own accounts. This enhances your audience's awareness and builds your reputation.

10.3 SOCIAL MEDIA

I began to use social media around 2006, driven by the need to monitor information leaks. Many of my colleagues had begun to share sensitive information about projects on emerging platforms such as Facebook, without realising that the platform is open. Later, when faced with the daunting task of doing PR in 40 countries without an advertising budget, I began to use the power of social media to reach people all over the globe, at no cost. In those days, no one in management cared about social media, so I was free to test and experiment. In short, I learned a lot.

First, I learned to be conservative. I myself was suspicious of the hype, so I only used established social media platforms and avoided the rest. There was a time that any self-respecting company had to have a profile on Second Life. The platform now barely has a pulse. There have been other local platforms, in many countries, to rise and fall in short order. I've avoided these and put effort in only a few solid ones. That said, not all of the Big Five are useful any longer for architectural PR purposes. Facebook, LinkedIn, Twitter and Instagram work fine. However, I have stopped using Pinterest as it is not as effective for what we wish to accomplish. Trends come and go, and a rumour now is that Facebook is 'over', but that hasn't been my experience. For us there are still 140,000 followers to reach and the number is growing. This is an indication that for MVRDV, it's still a relevant platform. TikTok is currently trending these days. Although we don't currently have a corporate presence on the platform, I will create one the moment that half the MVRDV staff are on TikTok. This is usually a clear indication that the platform is relevant for the industry.

If you wish to grow your business in China or Russia, I'd advise you to make an effort to engage with their protected social media platforms and be present. The mere potential of a viral posting on WeChat, Weibo or QQ, or VK and OK in Russia, can be incredible. Your business can flourish as a result. The viral news will ripple out and eventually the Western media will follow suit, so if you are doing PR in a foreign country, it can be valuable to check whether there are interesting local social media platforms to boost your business.

Social media is a fantastic means of communicating directly with your followers. These are likely to be a mix of peers, students, clients and fans, as well as an extended group of family and friends. At time of writing (May 2020), I can reach potentially – if the algorithm allows – 847,000 people, which is more than the print run of many newspapers; the potential to go viral could even multiply this number. This number is impressive and it took 11 years to build this following, but the question is, what do we do with this enormous potential?

Most social media allows you to check statistics and then provides important information indicating whether your social media activities are effective for your business. First of all, where are your followers located? Ideally, they'll be in places where you want to work. Secondly, are your followers of the decision-making age? Keep in mind that this can be a long-term investment. When I first created a Facebook presence for MVRDV, our followers were in their 30s. Any impact I had then was an investment in the future. Now, those followers are in their 40s and in more powerful, decision-making roles. Following the same logic, the future will indeed be bright. The 510,000 followers we have now on Instagram are young. In a decade, they will be decision-makers.

Assuming you have a small budget, and no allowance for an intrepid social media manager, how do you begin? You can go two ways: your way or adapt to the specific social media platform. 'Your way' is simply posting whatever you think is best, making no concessions to the platform, and just posting what you have. This can be a successful strategy. An adaptation would be a post that respects the character of the social media platform. There is a fine balance between serving the expectations of the readers on the platform and getting your message out there. Ideally, you may wish to find a way to bring the two strategies together. Keep in mind, social media is dynamic. You may wish to consult recent articles about each social media platform to stay informed of the latest developments. Roughly speaking, the rule of thumb is as follows: Facebook is personal, LinkedIn is business-oriented, Twitter is news-oriented and Instagram is image-based. To expand on what I mean:

Facebook: *Yay, we won the competition to build this cool new museum in Norwich! It's amazing!!! Check it out here: www.namearchitecturepractice.co.uk, accompanied by an image of yourself (a face) in a celebratory mood, maybe holding a model, or an image of the project.*

LinkedIn: *XXX Architects win Norwich Museum competition, a 10,000m² exhibition hall with a total investment of £45 million, completion planned for 2025. Read more at www.namearchitecturepractice.co.uk*

Instagram: *The post is just a small caption to a very aesthetic image of the project: Winning scheme for the Norwich Museum competition! #Norwich #Norwichmuseum #architecture #name-architecture-practice #name-engineer #name-client #name-otherconsultants*

Twitter: *We won the Norwich Museum competition, creating a new museum typology. Read the full press release at www.namearchitecturepractice.co.uk*

Each platform is different, and it follows that 'how' and 'what' you communicate will be different to suit the individual medium. This way, your approach can be tailored and sophisticated. In this image-dominant landscape, a visual of some kind is integral. In some cases, you can even use a small video clip. Test the results by posting something exclusively text-based, and something else that is a combination of text and imagery.

I would strongly advise you to use social media to generate more traffic to your website. Every social media post should link to relevant content on your website.

I have, as of May 2020, some 13,300 'friends' across my various personal accounts. I have met many of these individuals in person, but not all. I have a policy that I accept anyone who wants to connect with me, simply because I think it is impolite not to accept them. We remain strangers and 'friends' until they start to spam me. Only then will I 'cull' my list. In contrast, many of my colleagues have established strict parameters. Some say that they need to have at least met the individual in person. Others say that they need to have communicated at least via email. The more scrupulous among them want to keep their friend list as small and efficient as possible, to manage valuable contacts. You should do whatever works best for you. You may wish to google recent articles for advice, and inform yourself of the latest developments.

What's great about social media is that posts can rapidly evolve into a viral frenzy and your project can be catapulted into thousands or even millions of personal 'bubbles'. This can be both a blessing and a curse, as you may find yourself at the centre of an online maelstrom. (More on this in Chapter 10.6).

PRACTICAL TIPS REGARDING SOCIAL MEDIA

Research social media. This chapter only scratches the surface. The vast potential of social media is incredible. Read more about this in books or on websites. You can also get professional advice if you want to spend some money. This media can make your career if you use it effectively.

Check statistics. Check out the statistics on your platform's profile to see who is following you. Take action with your content if you are not reaching your target audience.

What do people expect? Consider your target group's interests and tailor the posts to them.

Experiment. Social media is immediate and you can check out the amount of views or likes that your post receives. Does your fanbase like construction images, renders or details best? You can give them more of what they want if you see that some kinds of posts have more success than others.

Link to your website. Given the fact that architects' websites are not the most visited sites on the internet, you can use social media as a 'feeder' to generate more traffic to your website. Sometimes clickbait might work. For example, 'We realised this building for less than £1,000 per m2; read here how we did this: www.namearchitecturepractice.co.uk/1000pounds.'

Tag your posts. If you tag your posts, you can expose them to an audience beyond those that subscribe to your account. The more precise the tag is, the more effective. For example, #architecture is sufficient, but *#museumarchitecture* is more precise. This will send the post to an interested audience of readers.

Five minutes a day can be enough. In the first few years, we never devoted more than five to ten minutes a day to social media, although it is possible to spend a vast amount of time and resources – many companies have a social media manager or even a team. Certainly smaller companies have the benefit that they can keep the investment lean and mean.

No-nos! Never curse, and avoid lengthy, nasty discussions. Never buy likes or friends. Never post anything remotely racist, homophobic, misogynistic or in any other way disrespectful. Never post while drunk. Remove tweets and posts that may embarrass you later. You might miss your chance to present at the Oscars.

10.4 TELEVISION

I have observed this quite often. When my colleagues have been on TV, the telephone rings, bringing all kinds of potential clients and requests to collaborate. In my experience, television is one of the most effective and immediate PR and business development mediums available.

And yet some people claim that television is a dying industry, as more and more channels share fewer and fewer viewers. Many people have stopped watching terrestrial television altogether, and are turning to websites such as BBC World for news, and streaming services such a Netflix or Amazon Prime for entertainment. Younger generations have turned to You Tube or TikTok.

Decision-makers aged 40 and older still watch television, so it is somewhat premature to dismiss the medium entirely. At the same time, using YouTube as a platform is an attractive alternative. You can reach large audiences without waiting for an invitation from the television media.

However, television still has influence. According to architect Carl Turner (see Case Study 7), whose private home construction was featured on the British TV show 'Grand Designs', it can make your career. Not only did it enhance the popularity of his practice, but also many people who contacted him said that they felt they knew him already. In addition to the exposure, he had customer buy-in even before meeting potential clients.

There are many challenges to consider. One is whether or not you have the ability to present yourself effectively on screen, and master your performance. Many Hollywood films feature architects as evil antagonists. For this reason, prejudices about the profession exist, and this lingers in the background of your TV performance. It might influence how you feel about presenting yourself. Personally, I hate being on television, and avoid it as much as I can. I fully understand how stressful it is when I send my colleagues to perform in talk shows or in documentaries. To master this better, they attend media training from time to time. This can include taking part in an interview in a real studio. I strongly advise that you do this if you are nervous.

Media trainers will advise you to prepare well. If you know what you want to say, you will feel much more relaxed. This is important for TV because insecurity can be visible to an audience. It is important to be calm, friendly and not to forget the essence of your message. Ensure that you have compelling arguments or an important position to share. Media trainers will help you remain in control of your story and support you with useful strategies. This is important as quite often in a talk show the conversation can derail and turn towards themes you might not want to discuss.

A very important factor to consider is how TV journalists work. If you can't afford to attend media training, or you have no time before the broadcast, ask for as much information as possible. If it is a talk show, it is important to ask who the other guests are and what position they'll present. Again, control is important here.

In terms of content, architecture is challenging due to its complexity. Television is a broad medium for all social classes and architects have a tendency to speak in industry jargon. For a television performance, you'll have greater impact when you use simple terms. To prepare, test your story with a friend or family member who is not an architect. It is also useful to test your story on an eight-year-old. Adapt your story so that the child understands it by using accessible vocabulary.

Optimism is also important to communicate when discussing your projects on TV. As much as you would like to avoid praising your work in press releases, television is a more personal medium, where you can afford to inspire the television audience with your enthusiasm and explain why your work is 'wonderful' or 'beautiful'. This way, non-architects follow your reasoning.

If the TV journalists and producers don't come a-knocking, and you're not successful in connecting with them (they receive a lot of requests and only have a mild interest in architecture), you may decide to make vlogs and become a YouTube architect (see Chapter 10.5).

PRACTICAL TIPS REGARDING TELEVISION

Prepare. This is important. Don't go to the recording studio unprepared. Try to test your story in advance. If you don't have the time or resources for media training, test your presentation with friends and family. Also, prepare for what you might say about critical questions or remarks. Imagine Prince Charles and his idea of modern architecture at the table. What would you say if he called your project a 'carbuncle'?

What is your message? Identify the essential information you want to convey and try to say it during the broadcast.

Use plain English. 'Archispeak' and long, complex sentences do not work on television unless the platform broadcasts a niche intellectual programme. The widely used architectural term 'volume' might mean something different to architects than to viewers. Be aware who your audience is.

Take two. If the broadcast is prerecorded, and you have the feeling that it just isn't working, ask the director to take the shot again.

Hate watching yourself? You've seen the broadcast and you absolutely hate it. Don't be surprised, many people hate watching themselves on television. Just ask a neutral person whether it's okay. Most of the time, it's not as bad as you think.

Have fun. Optimism and fun are inspiring and contagious, so try to be natural and positive on TV. Convey this enthusiasm to the viewers.

Appearance. Dress professionally, and try to avoid busy motifs on your clothing and other things that might distract from the message. Select a good background, for example the depth of your office. When interviewed on Zoom, etc., make sure that your eyes are on the same level as the camera and that the light is directed at you. You don't want to be a dark shadow that looks down on the audience.

10.5 VLOGS AND PODCASTS

Despite a growing number of channels, television remains an exclusive and competitive medium. However, thanks to YouTube, Vimeo and TikTok, you can create your own TV channel or radio station and record vlogs or produce podcasts.

Architects have not yet fully embraced the power of this new media. This might have something to do with a general disdain for self-promotion, or perhaps a shared scepticism for flashy trends. Don't let this dissuade you. We have a different target audience than the Kardashians, after all.

You can begin by making your own short film clips, perhaps even with something as simple as a smartphone. Take a few clips at a building site

Figure 10.5.1 *One of the most dynamic and fun architecture vlogs is #Donotsettle, whose vloggers Wahyu Pratomo and Kris Provoost are pictured here at Tianjin Binhai Library, Tianjin, China.*

visit. These short clips can become incredibly successful online and if they're captivating for an audience they can have viral potential, so are definitely worth your while. According to Statistica, moving images are attractive to all audiences.[4] Using video content, you stand a strong chance of capturing the attention of a large audience. It should not escape your notice that decision-makers fall into this cohort.

Your first question might be: is the architecture presented well in a low-tech and spontaneous movie clip? It's not easy to create high-quality, spontaneous video clips. Cinematography takes years to master, so how can you assume that you'll do it right? You won't at first. One solution is to relax and experiment. The wonder of online media is that you can test the waters with rapid iteration of content. By evaluating the number of views and the tone of the responses, you can determine what works and what doesn't, and the beauty of it all is that you can remove whatever is not successful.

Another question you might ask is whether self-promotion is acceptable. If it makes you uncomfortable, change the approach. A less direct means of contact is through existing architecture vlogs. Get in touch with them and ask if you can promote your projects and practice through their platform. As the producer of the platform, they can choose to filter out whatever they like, and it may be that they're not interested in your work. A list of current vlogs is below, but the medium moves quickly, so if these don't work for you, do some research to determine if there are more suitable vlogs for your work.

Your vlogging should adhere to the same guidelines as for other online media (see Chapter 10.3, 'No-Nos!'). Trends change often, so stay informed by reading the latest online articles on making great vlogs. In general, keep it short, personal, fun and powerful.

PRACTICAL TIPS REGARDING VLOGS AND PODCASTS

- **Be prepared.** Prepare for your vlog by writing a detailed script. Perhaps even write important lines on posters that 'actors' can read aloud. If a smart man like Barack Obama used a prompter, so can you.
- **Set up a channel.** Make your own channel on YouTube, or the more prestigious Vimeo. Alternatively, the young and hip TikTok might appeal to you.

Test. Make sure you have the right lighting and the right presenter. This is a visual medium, so respect the medium's rules in order to make a powerful visual impact.

Monitor and evaluate. Evaluate public reactions and, if need be, remove or update the video if it doesn't have the expected impact.

Drive traffic to the content. Most users on these kinds of social media platforms are too young to be decision-makers. You need to attract attention to the content via your website or relevant social media. If the production is successful, other online architecture media might pick it up. They are always looking for content that increases their readership.

Make it relevant. Self-promotion in and of itself is not interesting, so consider what it is about your content that might be useful for your audience and tailor it to make it relevant to them. Often architects are less star-struck and more looking for smart solutions that they can apply in their own work.

Check out how cool architecture vlogs are doing it. Shoot for the stars and try to get featured on one of these platforms: *Dezeen*, Chicago Architecture Foundation, Donotsettle (Figure 10.5.1), Harvard GSD, Architecture is a Good Idea, the Modmin, Arbuckle Industries, Photoshop Architect, Autodesk, Nick Senske, How to Architect and *ArchDaily*.[5]

Experiment. YouTube is a great place to experiment. You can take short and informal vlogs on a construction site, for example, or you can make more sophisticated productions and upload them online. Have a look at how Bjarke Ingels explains projects. He plays with a layer of virtual reality that is so impressive you forget all his Danish slang. Do whatever works for you, and generates positive reactions. If it doesn't generate the response you want, you can easily remove it from the platform, particularly if you use your own channel.

10.6 CRISIS COMMUNICATION AND THE OUTREACH THAT MIGHT PREVENT IT

Architects can sometimes find themselves in rather messy media-related situations. In 1979, parts of the roof of Kansas City's Kemper Arena, by Helmuth Jahn, collapsed. In 2005, OMA/Rem Koolhaas's CCTV tower, in Beijing, was presented in a book alongside Hitler's Chancellery discussing the Architecture of Power. In 2014, Zaha Hadid was embroiled in a press debate about the safety of construction workers building her Qatar World

Cup stadium. In 2016, the practice was in the thick of it again, when principal architect Patrik Schumacher spurred rioting in front of the ZHA London offices after making a controversial speech about public space and social housing. More recently, Bjarke Ingels faced a social media storm for appearing next to Brazil's right-wing president, Jair Bolsonaro, in a photograph. These can be terrifying moments. When architects find themselves in media-related trouble, it is most often because one of their projects has become the target of a political discussion, is at risk of termination, is victim to a public debate or at the centre of a political controversy.

These are the moments when a crisis communication plan will be useful. Nevertheless, it is hard to prepare for such a crisis, as it will likely hit at an inconvenient time and then demand all of your attention. The best advice is the old British slogan: keep calm and carry on. When emotions are high, the conversation often turns irrational. It is important that you stay calm, as hard as this might be. Situations like this can determine the future of your project. For this reason, it is important to be strategic and cautious, and to make decisions in combination with your client or the local authority, if applicable.

NEIGHBOURS RISE UP AGAINST THE PROJECT

In 2014, the City of Rotterdam decided to build a new 15,000m² art storage building in an inner-city park. The surrounding affluent neighbourhood, as well as a few nearby institutions (two museums and a hospital), rose up in protest against the proposed building location. This was a potential threat for a multimillion-euro donation the project had received, and nearly spelled its end. The city, the museum and the architects joined forces to create a crisis communication strategy. A number of information evenings were organised for concerned citizens. The learning curve was steep: with each new evening, chaos turned to order. Then came the city-wide poll to determine what citizens actually wanted. There were press conferences, lectures, information leaflets printed, a website built and a number of 'ambassadors' appointed to the project. These individuals were prominent Rotterdammers who supported the construction of the building. Meetings with the neighbouring institutions were organised, and the design was adapted where necessary. Now, the building is complete (Figure 10.6.1) and has considerable support. Countering the first negative outcry from a cohort of well-educated, influential and outspoken neighbours was integral to saving the project.[6]

Figure 10.6.1 *Depot Boijmans van Beuningen, Rotterdam, MVRDV, due to be completed in September 2021. In a park designed by Rem Koolhaas and Yves Brunier, the Depot Boijmans van Beuningen first received public scrutiny, after which a public participation process created wide support.*

Britain is much better organised when it comes to NIMBYs (Not in My Backyards), and adding a public participation expert to the proceedings is often part of a tendering procedure. If there is no demand or budget for this expert, but the project has the potential to cause friction, it might be a good idea to prepare for a crisis as much as possible. A great start to crisis communication is a quick Q&A to collect all possible negative responses. Then, you create solutions to these challenges in your public presentation. Organising public participation events, at the very least, can lead to a better design. Good timing is key for these events: when done too late, they may be perceived as fake participation. When organised well they give the neighbours an opportunity to voice their opinion. Options for the neighbours to choose from might also be a great strategy. However, be prepared for the possibility that they might choose the 'wrong' option. All options presented should be excellent solutions. If your project is under scrutiny, it makes sense to explain yourself and the project, so that the opposing side does not have the space to dominate.

SOCIAL MEDIA STORM

In 2011, MVRDV won a skyscraper project in Seoul, South Korea, which consisted of twin towers connected at their centre by a 'cloud', an 11-storey pixelated volume (Figure 10.6.2). After initial positive press in South Korea and Europe, the press reactions in the US were scathing. New Yorkers in particular felt that the project resembled the exploding World Trade Center, and that the design mocked the victims of this terrible tragedy. Fox News declared MVRDV the worst person of the day. Relatives of victims accused the architects of cruelty and disrespect. Facebook closed our account, and even fellow Dutch people sent threatening emails and called the practice, threatening to beat up the 'Bin Laden lovers'. Police organised protection on our behalf, and thereafter we explained the design steps factually, arguing

Figure 10.6.2 *The Cloud, Yongsan, South Korea, MVRDV, unrealised. The design evoked anger, mostly in the US, due to its perceived resemblance to the 9/11 explosions, while in South Korea the project was applauded and the connection was not made.*

that this bore no relation to 9/11. Given the volatile perception by the US media, we apologised for causing concern. We further organised BBC and national Dutch news coverage to explain our side of the story. However, the South Korean public was not so concerned with the controversy. They didn't see the resemblance, and the client organisation was even pleased with the publications. They even cited the old adage, 'There is no such thing as bad publicity'. After just one sleepless, stressful week, the controversy disappeared, but it left us with a few scars. Yet the client's logic proved strangely prophetic: only a few short months after, we began our first built project in New York.

Looking back on a week filled with emotions, threats and sleepless nights, we presented a calm and collected front to the outside world and demonstrated that we were determined to solve the issue. Valuable help came from PR experts in the US, who advised us as to how to address this particularly contentious challenge.[7]

ANTICIPATING CONTROVERSY AND PREPARING IN ADVANCE

Faced with possible controversy concerning a 3,500-unit neighbourhood transformation in Bordeaux, France, the city decided to follow a forward-thinking strategy. First, they announced the project at the 2014 Agora architecture biennale and made a website to provide further information. Then, they informed the civil servants and other stakeholders during workshops, to help influence the design. They then translated the project into an art sculpture and placed this sculpture on the main square in the city. Then, they organised public participation events, but were not able to contact all the neighbours. The architects took to bicycles, spontaneously visiting neighbours to chat over tea (Figure 10.6.3). Having been behind gates for many years, they opened the site to tours for interested citizens. The most pivotal moment was a presentation to UNESCO. The architects prepared two versions of the plan: an option that would be invisible from the city centre and a very visible plan. Confronted with the less appealing invisible option, UNESCO approved the visible version. Then, the city organised temporary site use to enliven the site before construction began (tours, markets, skating events and temporary use of buildings).[8]

There is a fine balance to apply in managing these situations, at least until you can solve a crisis through your own communication efforts. In the event of a project being in peril, the best strategy is a combination of stakeholders

Figure 10.6.3 *Having failed to meet the neighbours of an upcoming project in Bordeaux, MVRDV's Winy Maas (seated in the centre of this photograph) went to them by bike and had tea with some residents, who explained their objections to the project.*

who join forces to tackle the problem. I would advise that you enlist outside help in the form of a PR or public participation agency. There is often a moment when it may be necessary to call a lawyer. In this case, you must calculate and evaluate your chances for success, the costs of the lawyer and the potential profit of the project.

PRACTICAL TIPS FOR WHEN A SOCIAL MEDIA STORM STRIKES

Be prepared. Think about any possible problems the project presents, and formulate answers to them. Discuss these with your team to make sure you are all informed and on the same page. This can be as simple as a well-written Q&A. This might also help local politicians endorse your project.

Connect with PR experts and a lawyer in advance. Make sure that you have a great lawyer and that you know a PR specialist who you can consult in a hurry. In times of urgent crisis, it might be difficult to find the right person to help.

Share your position. When in crisis, keep calm and try to find a strategy that allows you to tell your side of the story.

Engage the public. Discuss with your client and/or the city you're working in whether a project is going to be difficult for the local community to accept, and evaluate whether you may wish to have a public consultation and implement a public participation strategy. Also, evaluate whether the controversy is likely to be insignificant or substantial. Will it jeopardise the project or not? If it does become a substantial threat, try to involve a professional agency.

10.7 OTHER MEDIA

Every text, image or drawing you produce, every meeting or encounter you have and everything your staff do has PR potential. Once you have drafted mission and vision statements (see Chapter 5) and developed a corporate identity (see Chapter 6), challenge yourself to see everything through this lens.

PRACTICAL TIPS REGARDING OTHER MEDIA

Use job advertisements to your advantage. These are PR moments, so approach them as such. Articulate your values, communicate your company culture and feature images of your work and graphic identity whenever possible. A job advertisement on Dezeen Jobs will have a captive audience, and it is not too expensive, so use this opportunity.

Adapt your language. If you are a happy architecture practice with a humane work ethic, make sure that all the language you use in your external communications reflects this. A formal employment contract with excessive legal jargon will likely not adhere to this philosophy. Alongside the guidance of a legal professional, adapt the language of the contract to align its voice and tone with your practice's identity.

Invest in your intranet. Internal communication is also an opportunity to articulate your practice's ethos. Instead of reprimanding your staff and telling them what not to do, change the approach to facilitate communal behavioural agreements. For example, change 'do not put personal items into the fridge' to 'this fridge is reserved for shared items only, in order to maintain our health'.

Craft a convincing elevator pitch. If you, or a member of your staff, are in the pub or at a family event, and people ask about your practice, ensure that you have a 30-second elevator pitch, which sincerely explains your raison d'être, at the ready. To facilitate this, pin up a one-liner at the coffee machine that articulates your company philosophy.

CHAPTER 11
LECTURES

Lectures provide a wonderful opportunity to inspire an audience with your work and philosophy. Take the audience on a journey through your world. Lectures usually run somewhere between 25 to 90 minutes. This also requires a clear storytelling strategy in order to captivate your audience and prevent boredom.

When invited to lecture, I suggest you evaluate the invitation with an open, yet critical, perspective. Ask yourself what it is going to bring you. Perhaps the lecture is an opportunity to address a whole audience of potential clients. If this is the case, agree. Architecture juries make an interesting audience, so this is also a good reason to agree. Maybe you receive an invitation to lecture in an exotic location that has always intrigued you, or perhaps other speakers are interesting and lecturing will provide an opportunity to network or, better still, learn something. On the other hand, the audience might not be interesting for your cause, but you want to practise public speaking. This is also a valid reason to accept.

Public speaking is a discipline that some master with natural ease, and others have to learn. It is heartening to know that you can acquire this skill. When I worked at OMA, there was a young, seemingly introverted Danish fellow who was not particularly chatty. Now he is a famous architect with his own successful practice, and stuns audiences all over the world with his enthusiastic and perfectly composed lectures. This architect is Bjarke Ingels.

I give up to 40 lectures a year, and two thirds of these lead to contacts with potential clients. It is a rather open-ended exercise. Often lectures that seem to have no real acquisition value result in fantastic opportunities. A potential client might be sitting in the audience and might approach you immediately after your lecture, or perhaps a local architect might want to collaborate.

A good rule of thumb is to talk about your practice's design approach through images. Support the imagery with a clear storyline. This must be a story that communicates your passion and enthusiasm for your work and your philosophy, and features your work at its best. Weave anecdotes into your story wherever appropriate and use these to offer a quick change in pace in your storyline, and to captivate your listeners.

Figure 11.1 *Even if you lecture many times, stage fright can hit you. It's not necessarily a bad thing; it can signal that you need to be sharp. Pictured speaking in this photograph is the author, Jan Knikker.*

Adapt your lecture to your audience. If you receive an invitation to speak at a tourism conference, for example, try to make your lecture content relevant. Do not take the easy route and arrive with a standard, out-of-the-box lecture. Put your content within the context of the conference, making it much more relevant to the audience. Do your due diligence and ask the organiser what the composition of the audience will be, to tailor your content and approach to their particular interests. In general, if your audience is comprised of architects, they might be interested in innovative solutions, building details and in mistakes you've made, problems you've encountered and how you overcame them. On the other hand, if your audience is made of civil servants, they might want to hear about solutions regarding fire regulations or guidelines for urban design. If project developers are in your audience, they might be keen to understand the financial side of your project work, as well as how well your buildings perform. For example, I recently addressed an audience of 1,100 IT specialists, so I teased out relevant details regarding BIM (Building Information Modelling) and scripting in all of the projects I discussed.

Another good rule of thumb is to respect time limits. Quite often, I experience lectures at conferences that run beyond their allotted time, and the architect speaking must abruptly cut their lecture short. This can occasionally result in a nasty public scrimmage, which does not reflect well on the speaker. The audience understands that poor preparation is to blame. If this happens, be polite, but try preventing it from happening in the first place through conscientious preparation. Respect time limits and prepare your lecture with these parameters clearly in mind. Take time to rehearse at home, in order to evaluate your running time. If necessary, shorten it while ensuring that you maintain a lively pace. Many conferences insist on a 25-minute lecture timeframe. This serves as a clear limitation to your preparation, and helps you to define priorities. Anything worth explaining can certainly fit into a 25-minute lecture, with a clear storyline.

Despite the fact that I frequently lecture (Figure 11.1), I still succumb to stage fright. Minutes before I step on stage, my throat tightens and I start to perspire nervously. I have come to understand that this is a natural process and that it releases adrenaline. I am now so accustomed to it that I actually worry if I don't get stage fright, and wonder if I will be as sharp and awake as I need to be. I usually receive good feedback from my lectures (also in anonymous surveys), so it is clear that people do not know how frightened or nervous I may be. Don't worry too much about stage fright. It's part of the process. When I gave a lecture in front of 2,600 people at a food conference, I was so frightened that I wanted to share this with the audience, so I started by saying, 'There are so many of you, I think I might faint at any minute because I am so nervous.' This immediately disarmed the audience and they laughed along with me; thereafter, the lecture proceeded with ease.

Last but not least, a lecture is a great PR moment but it should not be a PR story. Make it a personal account, show your passion and be authentic. Also, be human. This is especially important in front of peers, as you should not only present achievements but also endeavour to share your mistakes and missteps. Share what you've learned as a result, and how you have overcome challenges. This makes for a much more dynamic lecture. If you consider how the storyline of a play or film unfolds, begin by introducing a challenging situation, then discuss the means of approach to the challenges through the project, pepper this storyline with anecdotes of minor challenges and then arrive at a climactic conclusion.

PRACTICAL TIPS REGARDING LECTURES

Analyse the audience and the theme. Ask the lecture organiser who your expected audience is and what they might want to hear from you. Profile your audience. Discover what their interests are, and adapt your story without losing sight of what you want to convey.

Define your storyline. Create a storyline that is interesting and will capture your audience's attention. If you don't want to deliver a PR story, also talk about new insights, mistakes and problems.

Consider payment terms. A lecture will take potentially 12 to 20 hours of preparation time and travel. How do you generate value from this? This should not be a price for your actual services. You lecture in exchange for free PR, and you should view your efforts from this perspective. However, do consider the potential value the experience offers you and your practice. If it costs you £2,000 in lost hours, will the spin-off from this lecture return the investment? As a basic rule, I expect the organisation to pay for travel and accommodation. We sell architecture, not lectures, so each additional fee is welcome, but do not base your decision on the fee offer, if there is one. Academic lectures are rarely worth the investment in terms of acquisition, so in this case request that they cover travel and accommodation and take on the responsibility of educating the next generation. View this as an honour. Agree to dinner with the organisation if they offer it, as this often leads to friendships and valuable new business or academic relationships.

Bait events. Sometimes architects' lectures bait peers to attend a commercial event such as a construction fair. In this case, you might consider requesting a higher fee, and thinking very strategically about what you want to achieve. If the fair is potentially interesting, you may wish to attend.

Consider available technical equipment in your planning. Ask organisers about the technical equipment available: is there a microphone, computer, screen, remote control, etc.? If you cannot send the lecture well in advance, ensure that you send another file from the same machine to the organisation to test that it works.

Pack your lecture on a USB stick. Save your lecture on both your computer and on a USB stick. Your laptop may possess an uncanny ability to die just before a big lecture, and your lecture with it.

Don't forget your sense of humour. You might want to open with a friendly joke. This will help you to establish an immediate rapport with your audience.

Be prepared for striking cultural differences. In the south of Europe, audiences can be quite vivid and interactive, even applauding in the middle of the lecture. However, in Scandinavia, your audience might receive the same joke with an icy silence. Once, after a lecture in Helsinki without any audience interaction, a fellow from the audience approached me and said, with a rather grim facial expression, 'It was a great lecture, you changed my life, thank you so much.'

Ignore sleepers. Pay no mind to sleepers and phone-checkers, unless these are the majority of your audience. Inevitably, you will encounter audience members who fall asleep, and some others who compulsively check their phone. No matter, this is normal. However, if half the audience falls asleep, it's either that you have driven them to slumber, or jet lag taking its toll, or poor air and temperature control in the lecture hall. If in doubt, request a frank review from the organisers.

Pursue training. If public speaking continues to be a challenge, invest in training. This will make life much easier for you personally, as trainers can respond to your personal issues and help you to become more confident and effective.

Enlist other speakers. If you hate lecturing and do not have enough time, enlist other colleagues and staff. Ensure that they represent your practice positively. Perhaps encourage them to rehearse by giving a lunch-and-learn presentation for your office.

Combine PR and BD. Imagine that a lecture organisation invites you to lecture in a location where you would like to work. Why not combine the trip with some business development meetings and try to connect with local architects and developers to work with in future? Also, ask the lecture organisation to invite people from organisations that you would like to be present at the lecture.

Work on your presentation skills. Speak clearly. Do not look down but clearly address the audience by looking at them with all the confidence you have in you. Stand still and do not pace around like a wild animal in a cage. Address the audience and not the presentation screen; this is a very common mistake.

Language. When presenting in a language that does not come easily for you, practise and practise some more. Get rid of any words you find complicated. In general, make sure you use a language that your audience will understand (neither too complex nor too simplistic).

Rehearse your lecture. We prepare for all kinds of things in life, so also take time to prepare for a lecture. I often rehearse the lecture in the hotel room to know how long it will be.

Don't panic. Exercise flexibility, and aim to problem solve on the fly, if your projector quits or your computer fails. Once, while lecturing about Markthal Rotterdam, my projector quit. I improvised without the aid of images, and the audience still loved it. I discovered a latent talent for pantomime, by sketching building details in the air. Another time, I lost my PowerPoint and proceeded to give the lecture entirely based on our website, browsing through, googling and explaining the work as I went. More often than not, your audience will appreciate your effort, and enjoy the impromptu performance.

CHAPTER 12
AWARDS

One fundamental truth in marketing, regardless of the sector you work in, is that consumers like to buy award-winning products. Paradoxically, unlike other approaches I've highlighted, this is one part of marketing that architects actually do seem to enjoy, and many have mastered. Awards are a real industry when you discover that often you have to pay for them. The more media attention the awards generate, the more expensive they are. With the exception of a few prestigious ones, the days of passively receiving an award have long since passed, so the 'business' of pursuing them represents both a financial investment and an important opportunity. I ensure that each of our completed projects receives an award by strategically submitting projects in categories for contests where they stand a strong chance of winning.

The top tier of the architecture award food chain includes the Pritzker Prize, the Stirling Prize, the Praemium Imperiale, the Mies van der Rohe Award and the Aga Khan Award for Architecture. Very little can be done to secure nomination for these awards; they are a genuine honour, and receiving them is a mark of significant recognition within the architectural community.

However, you have greater control (by strategically applying) over award organisations like WAN, Red Dot or the German Design Award, which are much more accessible, but at a cost. There are also numerous international awards in various countries that you can choose to pursue. Generally speaking, it is wise to consider the award's particular added value before applying. Try to understand whether the award will be useful from a PR and BD perspective, and obtain a clear picture of how much pursuing it will cost you. Many awards ask for an entrance fee, and then a second fee if you win. The WAN awards are very popular with architects, and cost you roughly £400 to £600, and a bit more if you're shortlisted, for a ticket to the award ceremony. A Red Dot Award will cost around £800 to enter and, if successful, there are additional costs for the publication and exhibition. The special appeal and PR value these awards offer is their prestige, as well as their recognition with clients. Chinese clients, for example, love to see that your projects have won a German award. In Chinese tenders, a list of awards is often a core requirement. To that end, it is advisable to ensure that each realised building has at least one award.

Awards won through public voting are an important honour to aspire to because they have the potential to be more genuine, but also because they can serve as a test to determine how well you can generate your own publicity. In the past, the MVRDV PR staff would share public voting polls on social media and walk around the office persuading each staff member to complete the poll. A mere 200 votes from within your practice might seem pithy, but this can make a difference, so in this respect, larger offices have a real advantage. So there is no shame in asking your extended friends and family for help to win. Playing it right with a good social media campaign can deliver the results you want.

If you receive an award, ensure that you display it somewhere on your office walls to capture the attention of incoming clients. Announce any awards on your media channels and attach them to all communication material associated with the project.

PRACTICAL TIPS REGARDING AWARDS

Assess the value of the award. Do the costs to participate and the chances of winning make sense? Will your clients be impressed? Is this part of your PR strategy? Awards are a commercial business, and you must consider this. It is an honour to have been selected, as much as it is sales targeting.

Find out who is on the jury. If the jury is comprised of experts not in favour of your brand or your architectural style, it may not be wise to compete. Many architectural experts are flexible and friendly, but there are also dogmatic old stodges who would not award a style alien to their own work. Do your due diligence and find out who will be evaluating your work.

So, you've won the award. Should you attend the award ceremony? Congratulations! Now think about whether or not you will go to the award ceremony. If possible, make some enquiries in your network to determine whether other award-winners think it worthwhile to attend.

Think of it as a tender. Many awards require you to present the work in such a way that the layout is equal for each project. Remember that juries see hundreds of entries. The background work you do is comparable to that of a tender. How can you make your entry relevant and distinct? Sending the standard marketing material is not sufficient. Perhaps you could consider other parameters the jury might apply to their assessment, and make it easy for them to see this value in your project by clearly illustrating these parameters. It is certainly not rocket science, but there is an art. For a sustainability award, it is obvious that you should illustrate your project's sustainable features.

CHAPTER 13
YOUR PRODUCT IN THE PICTURE

Architecture is a visual and tactile discipline. If your main means of production is software, you might consider all the other manifestations of your work as translations of your core business. You can also use 2D drawings and 3D models to present your work; however, all other materials, texts, images, diagrams, books, photographs, renders, models and collages are products that serve to enhance the communication of design ideas to clients and stakeholders. How you approach the translation of ideas into these different media available will define how the world experiences you, and your work. Most architects do this well and rather intuitively. However, you might consider being intentional about how your ideas are visualised and implementing a thoughtful strategy to ensure that this communication adheres to your philosophy, beliefs and visual identity.

Your marketing efforts begin at the drawing level. To this end, it is important for your practice to develop an overall style of content output in line with the architecture you produce. A traditional architecture practice might wish to work with renders that look like hand drawings, and wooden models, while an edgy parametric practice might use 3D prints and animations.

The next question is whether or not you want to impose a uniform style to communicate to all clients, or whether you can adjust your style to reach certain client typologies, different press or stakeholders in order to speak to their respective needs. Over the next few subchapters, I will discuss the various manifestations of the architectural drawing (or 3D model).

13.1 THE DRAWING

It has surprised me to discover that architects are sometimes not able to read a technical drawing made by other architects. If these individuals, the trained professionals that they are, cannot understand a 2D drawing, why continue to use this medium as a communication tool with clients? How can it possibly be an effective means of communication?

I am not an architect myself, so I have remained blissfully incompetent when reading architectural drawings. I frequently ask architects to explain items on the drawing to me, only to discover that they themselves are puzzled by my questions:

Architect: I think this is a ramp, or no, maybe a void? I'm not sure.
Me: But you've realised this building?
Architect: Yeah, but this is like five years ago.

So imagine that you are not an architect, have never had formal technical education and must now make sense of black lines on white paper, to imagine a building. This is where 'sales drawings' are important. They are an effective communication tool, as they make the building understandable, though they are far from what architects work with to actually produce drawings for construction purposes. They are a unique representation.

Think about how people will experience an architect's typical 'sales' drawings: boxes indicating an apartment, and interior spaces, a bedroom, a bed, maybe a couch for scale. To make this tangible, add colour, pillows, bedding and all manner of household accessories to create a cartoon-like version of an apartment, viewed from a bird's-eye perspective. The location of the television, the sofa cushions, tables, chairs and other furnishings is clear, and clients see a fully furnished illustration. This helps them understand the scale of rooms, and for those with little experience with architectural drawing, imagine themselves in the space (Figures 13.1.1–4).

On the other side of the spectrum are design and construction industry peers. For an indication of what is required to communicate to this audience, look at magazines such as *Detail* or *El Croquis*. These publications feature details and drawings that illustrate a certain level of design complexity, with smart solutions that appeal to an architectural audience alone. I once had 26,000 views on a LinkedIn post when I shared a detail of an outdoor balcony flowerbed. It irritated me that so many people claimed trees could not grow on buildings, so I shared a technical detail that demonstrated how this was possible. It received quite a bit of traction. This is due in no small part to the fact that many people in my network are architects, and they are particularly interested in making details like this possible in their own projects.

Appreciate the platform that quality publications featuring architectural drawings and technical details provide. There are so few, and they enhance

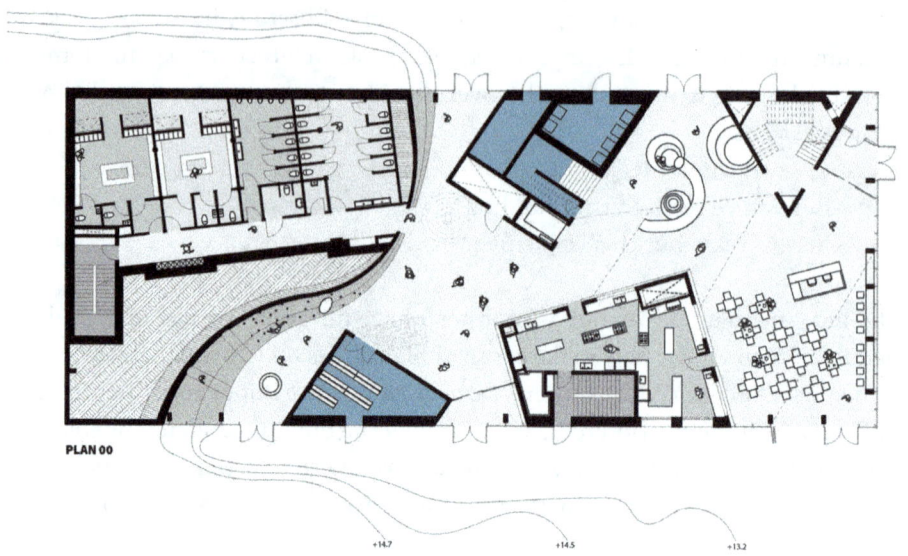

Figure 13.1.1 *KUBE, House of Movement, Copenhagen, MVRDV and ADEPT. The use of furniture and colour in plans helps non-architects to understand the plans better, especially in terms of scale and function.*

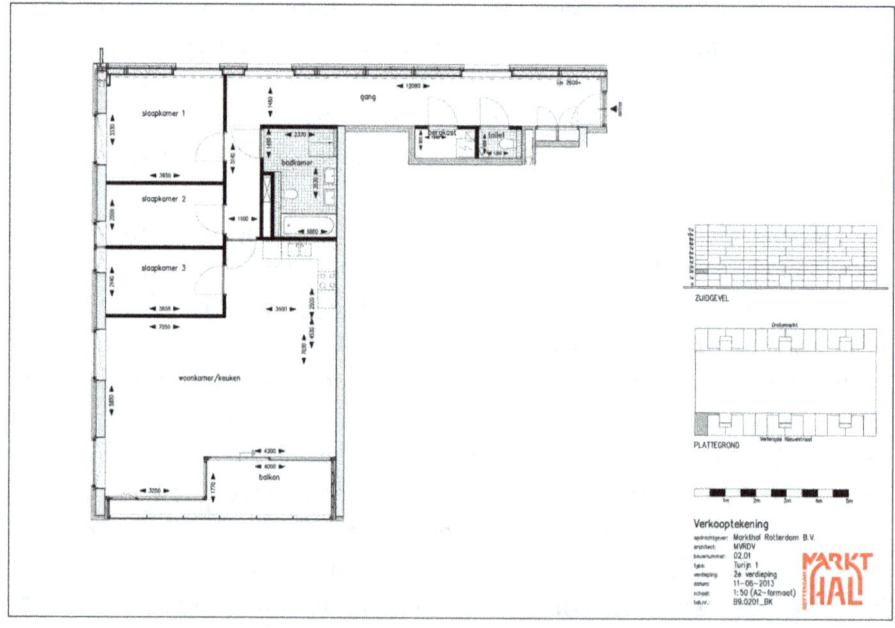

Figures 13.1.2–4 *Markthal Rotterdam, MVRDV. So-called sales drawings, progressing from technical to more marketing-based. The coloured version is the most understandable for consumers looking into buying an apartment.*

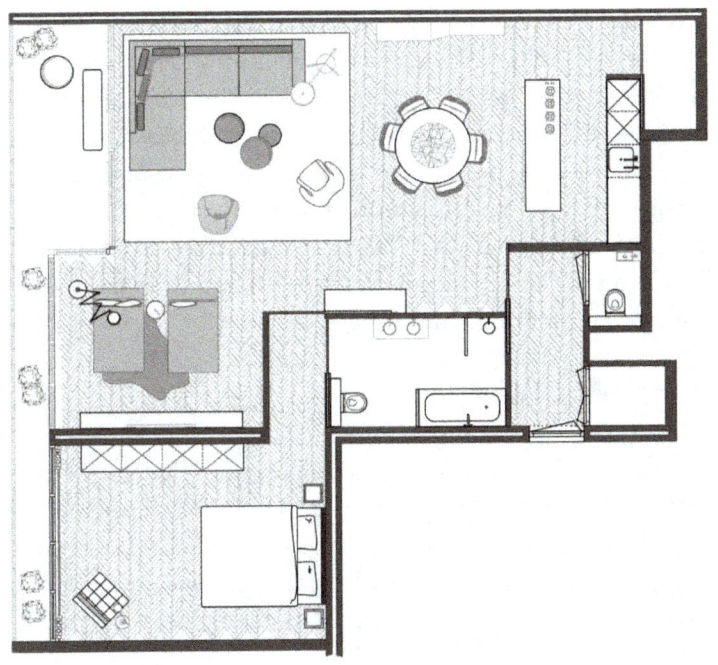

13. YOUR PRODUCT IN THE PICTURE

professional practice, as they serve as a means of sharing knowledge across the discipline. Despite the additional work that a publication of this nature involves, I would agree to participate and pursue publication. It is heartening that platforms like this still exist, and they will not only enhance the bank of knowledge in the discipline, but also help enhance your practice's recognition with peers. Forgive me for painting the purity of architectural knowledge sharing with a PR brush. As much as a contribution like this demonstrates dedication to the enhancement of the discipline, there is an opportunity for practice promotion. This is PR, after all.

PRACTICAL TIPS REGARDING DRAWINGS

Make your material readable. Think about your audience. If you think that the jury or the readers of the publication many not understand your drawings due to their complexity, remove technical features and, if necessary, furnish them to make spaces more tangible. I would suggest that you consider your audience's technical capacities as low. Improve accessibility with a clean or furnished drawing that is easy to understand.

Test your content on non-technical people. Test legibility again by asking your eight-year-old nephew, or anyone not related to your discipline, if they can find the bedroom on the drawing. If they can, you've done alright.

Illustrate potential client aspirations. When furnishing a drawing, avoid making it exceedingly specific. Instead, use a high-end-looking but familiar interior set-up. This means placing couches and armchairs facing a television. People want to buy a new home to enhance their lifestyle, so there is always some element of aspiration. If the living room is large, furnish it, in addition to basic elements, with perhaps a grand piano. This is an example of an aspiring element that also serves to illustrate the scale of the room.

Technical drawings and 3D sections. These kinds of illustrations demonstrate craftsmanship and spatial qualities of your designs. Try to publish them in peer magazines whenever possible.

13.2 THE RENDER

Unless you're an architect, you might experience some difficulty in understanding an architectural drawing or section. For this reason, the photorealistic render has become an almost indispensable communication tool for architects. It is a crucial means of sharing architectural ideas with clients and capturing the public's imagination. Having lost a competition due to less-than-inspiring imagery, I learned this the hard way. According to the client, we had a better project than the competition, but they won because their renders were vibrant and upbeat. Our renders were not. Another critical learning opportunity arose when a client confessed that our architectural illustrations made him sad, and led him to question whether the spaces we'd designed were even safe. The stylish grey and abstract interior sketches we'd presented conjured thoughts of mugging rather than the sleek sophistication we'd intended. It was through these hard knocks that we learned the value of the photorealistic render, as well as an essential ingredient: the 'happiness filter'. This is a term we use for adorning images with the right kind of people, objects and activities. After a while, we spent so much money contracting this service outside the office, we could afford our first render artist. Today, we have formalised this whole process into our design development activities and, to support this, have an in-house render studio with eight architect-artists.

The photorealistic render has a controversial reputation: it is an advertisement and propaganda tool, and can be a purveyor of fraudulence when used deceitfully. More often than not, it is a wonderful vision of the future that captures our imagination. This power lies in its representation of a highly realistic vision. Sometimes renders are crafted with such precision that it is almost impossible to say whether the project has in fact been built or is still in the conceptual phase. With this technological possibility comes a great responsibility. For example, the manipulation of an artistic rendering of a new high-rise district in The Hague featured buildings of a lower height profile than planned. The city councillor held responsible for the deceit stepped down after a local newspaper made the discovery.

It is important to make renders that can stand the test of a comparison with the completed building. Remember that the render is a promise; do not show what you cannot realise. To this end, it can be beneficial to be slightly vague or abstract in the illustration. For example, present an undefined façade

Figure 13.2.1 and 13.2.2 *A render is supposed to create identification for the spectator to engender support for the project. In many renders, however, the perspective and the selected people make it hard to identify with. The perspective looks inward, the people are shown from behind and make it difficult for the spectator to 'participate'. The action is in the image (in the orange section); the spectator is an outsider.*

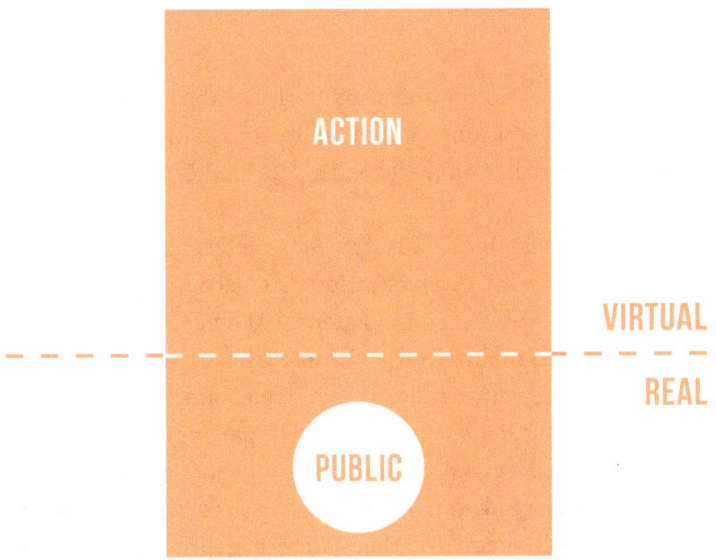

Figure 13.2.3 and 13.2.4 *More engaging for the spectator are renders where the action happens in a space that ends 'behind' the spectator. The people in the render look towards the spectator and they share a space (the orange box, which in this case is everywhere), blurring the line between virtual and real. The spectator is an active part of the action. This creates more potential for support – the spectator can imagine walking inside the space.*

material or perhaps simply do not feature the building façade that is still unfinished, or in debate.

Renders are an excellent communication tool, but the challenge lies in finding a balance between concept and reality and using the tool honestly, while still being sales oriented (Figures 13.2.1–13.2.4).

Without the luxury of in-house services, most architects must rely on external render studios. This collaboration can be challenging because the impact of the artistic impression is so great that a very close collaboration is necessary in order to maintain the vision of the architect in the best way possible. When looking for a render studio, style, budget and delivery time must weigh in balance. Of all of these, style, in particular, is crucial. Many inexpensive render firms can produce images in short order, but these tend to be bland and impersonal. You get what you pay for. At the other end of the price and quality spectrum, there are firms with definitive artistic presentation. One of the best render studios in the market is MIR, an award-winning office renowned for creating dramatic weather conditions, and for wonderfully precise photorealistic work. If you prefer your work awash with sunlight and happy children, they might not be the right studio. Endeavour to find one that aligns with your work, your philosophy and your particular client's expectations. This will ensure a more fluid creative process, and keep conceptual expectations in line.

If you simply do not have the budget and you must work with the first 3D image your select rendering engine inside the practice produces, you can still make compelling images with enhancements in Photoshop. Consider your render as an advertisement for your project. This can also support the investment of working with a render firm. In generating an image of the project presented in a specific way, you are selling a lifestyle and the future success of your work. If you want to let your client know that the home you design is warm and inviting, choose warm furnishings and a warm material palette for the interior. If you want your client to believe that the shop you are designing will be a commercial success, create a bustling atmosphere, with shoppers carrying filled shopping bags in the render. Identification is a strong advertisement tool, so consider how your client and the public want to see themselves. To this end, consider what the building will bring in terms of aspiration or social events and then illustrate this in the image so that your audience can identify (Figures 13.2.5 and 13.2.6). In Chinese

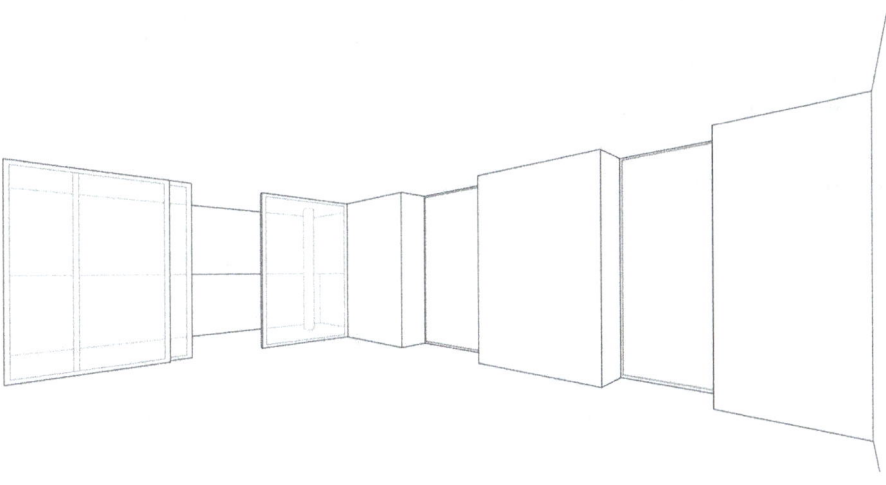

Figure 13.2.5 and 13.2.6 *Often renders sell a lifestyle in addition to the architecture. This interior render is dominated by a high-end interior, an attractive inhabitant and a wide view. If we bring the image back to its structure, there is little architecture to see but a corner of a room with some windows. In this kind of image the aspirational 'dressing' is essential. The fact that the render artist has chosen a woman is not sexist, but smart marketing: women tend to identify less easily with men in advertisements (men identify equally with both sexes). The render artist is ensuring the widest possible market identifies with the image.*

advertisements, British tea companies and American car manufacturers feature their products with Big Ben and the Grand Canyon to create an aura of origin, but the people in these advertisements are Chinese – because they are selling to the Chinese, not to British or American people.

Style-wise I am not necessarily in favour of the photorealistic render, because it is a commercialised illustration of the architectural project as opposed to the visceral physical model, or more conceptual artistic collage. Nevertheless, the tool is irreplaceable and something we must use in order to be commercially successful, by convincing our clients and the public of the strength of our architecture. Because the language of advertising is ubiquitous, we must use this language to communicate to the public, who, according to digital marketing experts, 'are exposed to around 4,000 to 10,000 ads each day'.[1] Photorealistic rendering is part of this visual culture and has a great potential to influence the public, who generally cannot read traditional architectural drawings (Figures 13.2.7–8).

Looking beyond photorealistic rendering, we have also begun to communicate architectural concepts using virtual reality technology with increasingly realistic furnishing and materialisation. Perhaps the virtual vignette will soon replace the photorealistic render altogether.

PRACTICAL TIPS REGARDING RENDERS

Think about the story you want to tell. This helps when selecting the right angles, weather, style, light and 'dressings' with people, furniture and activities.

Select the render studio wisely. The images they produce define the way that the public and your clients evaluate your creation.

Consolidate feedback. Provide feedback at critical, predetermined moments. Render studios are often pressed for time just before the deadline. In these moments, they are less willing to interact with you and want to ensure that their workflow is efficient. To this end, consider the render carefully at these predetermined moments to make sure you're commenting on everything. Renders do not improve in the ping-pong between many parties, or by making massive changes at the last minute.

You are the client. Keep in mind that many render studios have their own style, but you are the client and they are obliged to tell the visual story of your project in the manner you commission them to. That said, respect them for their expertise in terms of image composition. It may

Figure 13.2.7 *Render studio Luxigon made this version of the entry to the Lille Hotel School for MVRDV. They published this on their website.*

Figure 13.2.8 *MVRDV wanted the render to have more life and openings. The building to the right is now pleasant and not ridden with black holes. The sky, however, remains in an apocalyptic colour.*

Figure 13.2.9 *MVRDV's PR studio decided to change the render, which now has a sunnier sky.*

Figure 13.2.10 *Identification is an essential trait of marketing. Foreign brands from Europe or America use Chinese models in their advertisements in China to increase the potential identification by the public. You can do this in your renders by selecting the right kind of users for your projects.*

help to show an example of a render you used successfully for an earlier submission, to create clarity on your expectations.

Deliver what you promise. Be careful when featuring expensive façade materials on a published render. If you execute the building with less expensive or sophisticated materials, you haven't fulfilled the promise your imagery conjured. In the event that the design changes, it is best to make new renders if the budget allows, in order to prepare the public for the alteration. This prevents the disappointment that ensues when you've anchored a wonderful vision in the hearts and minds of the public and then underdelivered in the realised building.

Remember: contrast is key. Dressing a home with red accessories, even if it is a minimalist home, raises the interest of potential online buyers by up to 30%, according to Dutch homebuyers' website Funda.

Speak to your audience. Identification increases with the right people and activities in your imagery (Figure 13.2.4). Selecting the wrong ones can be fatal. There is an obvious difference between people in different countries, but also in different users of different buildings. Patrons of a hip temporary workspace in Shoreditch will differ from those in a

retirement home in Dorchester. Ask yourself whether the people and the furniture are the right choice. Some element of aspiration can be welcome. With this, balance is key. A Porsche in front of a housing project with affordable or subsidised housing might communicate shady activity, while second-hand cars might, on the other hand, be discriminatory.
- **Remember: your render is a promise.** Online discussions on *Dezeen* can be merciless for renders with trees on roofs that are too large, or other unbelievable features.
- **Make use of the vast amount of resources online.** If you make your own renders, there are catalogues of people and objects for sale online that can enhance your visual imagery and save you a considerable amount of time.
- **Balance the books.** You might think that establishing an in-house render team is only for larger studios, but the business model is simple. The moment you spend more money on renders on a monthly basis than an in-house artist would earn, you can begin.

13.3 COLLAGES AND HAND DRAWINGS

The collage and the hand drawing were the Photoshop before Adobe software existed. In the past, architects such as Le Corbusier and Mies van der Rohe made the collage illustration popular, using these to make qualities of the design tangible. Using people and furniture, these collages illustrate how spaces can be loved, used and, as a result, successful.

There are architects today who nostalgically cling to these presentation forms because they suit their work and identity. This is wonderful if it works, and there are excellent examples of practices which successfully communicate using these tools, but there are some compelling arguments against using this particular kind of imagery.

I learned this the hard way. A Russian client once wanted a design for a transformation of New Holland Island, in St Petersburg, and we created a plan that was exactly what they wanted. In the words of the client, we read his mind. We chose to illustrate the plan with artistic collages (Figure 13.3.1), and the client particularly appreciated these qualities. Then he polled the general public for their opinion, who selected a competing plan, which presented standard renders with hot-air balloons, happy kids and colourful

Figure 13.3.1 *Collage of New Holland Island, St Petersburg, Russia, MVRDV. Using a collage instead of a render cost MVRDV the competition win in this prestigious transformation project.*

picnics (Figure 13.3.2). Understanding our audience, we should have created understandable renders for the public. As much as an abstract collage was useful to convince the client, it was too esoteric for a public audience to digest.

Nevertheless, collages are a wonderful tool that add quality and artistic character to your design ideas. They are best for projects that require a certain whimsy in their illustration. When choosing whether to render or collage, think carefully about your audience and the tactics you must employ to reach them. One example of making the wrong assumptions is in the West Kowloon Cultural District competition. The winning proposal by Foster + Partners relies heavily on renders, as well as its urban plan, which provides a lush new green space in Hong Kong (Figures 13.3.3 and 13.3.4). In contrast, the OMA proposal illustrates a wonderfully artistic quirkiness. Foster won the competition, and while it goes too far to attribute this only to the use of renders versus collages, it does seem plausible that this is at least partly to blame. The differences between the two plans are marked, and their respective use of either collage or render influences the overall presentation. Foster's renders illustrate a project that the public can understand. Furthermore, they illustrate a familiar scene that includes a

Figure 13.3.2 *Render of New Holland Island, St Petersburg, Russia, WORKac. The winner of the New Holland Island competition, WORKac, made renders which won the hearts of the Russian public.*

day in the life of the area's future use. The public can rely on these scenes to imagine how they'll use the park themselves. On the other hand, the OMA proposal is abstract, leaving elements of the master-planning phase more open to the imagination. Whatever your choice, you need to be certain that you select the right quality of presentation. The fact that renders are easier to understand, are ubiquitous and that audiences are accustomed to them presents a strong case for their use.

A great example of the use of collages is the portfolio of Turner Works (see Case Study 7). In addition to permanent projects, this multidisciplinary group transforms factories, containers and even parking garages into temporary spaces. To show this potential, they often use incredibly effective collages that fully support the temporary and slightly alternative-creative character of each project. Here, the collage presents the project in an artistic way, which proves to be the right communication for future users of these spaces: often millennials with a taste for the authentic (Figure 13.3.5).

In an age of computer-aided design, hand drawings can lend a feeling of quality and craftsmanship to a project. For example, for a tower with a

Figure 13.3.3 *Render of West Kowloon Cultural District, Hong Kong, by Foster + Partners.*

Figure 13.3.4 *Front page of the Foster Times, issued 20 August 2010 by Foster + Partners.*

Figure 13.3.5 *Collage for Elephant Arcade, in London, by Turner Works.*

rhomboid façade in Taiwan, actually designed in BIM, an Italian architect began by drawing the shape in ink with a Montblanc pen, demonstrating how artistic the creative process is. This rhomboid sketch represented the project on the cover of its sales magazine.

Another appeal of hand drawings is their sketchy character. These make the project look less intimidating, and harmlessly unfixed. Consider the friendly drawings that promoted Damien Hirst's housing project, a mediocre urban plan softened by a soft watercolour green and hand-drawn axonometric illustrations. At best, these illustrate a community still in a sketch phase, still up for debate and alteration. These can be manipulative when used to make a project seem less controversial, or to downplay the real scale of a project.

Whichever you choose – render, hand drawing or collage – furnish and accessorise them with a complementary selection of people, events and objects. Even in a fast hand sketch of a shopping centre, for example, illustrate shoppers with shopping bags. For a museum collage, cut out interesting visitors and renowned art pieces. These media are rich and allow for creative and artistic work, so max out their capabilities with appropriate whimsical illustration.

PRACTICAL TIPS REGARDING COLLAGES AND HAND DRAWINGS

If your client or the audience is 'artsy', use collages. Artistic and intellectual audiences have a real appreciation for this kind of representation. These may also appeal to a niche market, such as the users of temporary creative spaces, who are a great audience for collages. However, don't forget that a render is easy to understand and provides a more realistic presentation of the project. Few people have a clear understanding of design in the abstraction of a collage.

If your context is a public participation process, use sketches. Especially in stakeholder or public participation processes, hand drawings or collages illustrate the temporal character of the work. You can communicate that the project is not yet finalised, and that the public can change the design by participating.

Communicate craftsmanship with hand drawings. In sales, hand drawings by genius architects create a sense of craftsmanship for potential buyers. This works on all levels, from end consumers who want to buy apartments crafted by architectural insight, to corporate clients who want to see the same.

Consider client aspirations in selecting the presentation method. If using collages and hand drawings, illustrate a clear argument for why your design works well. This could mean that for a sober Swiss client you add few additional illustrative features, and for an opulent Italian designer store, you apply a rich assemblage of people and furniture. Ensure that the features you draw out in the collage or hand drawing communicate the strengths of your project, and illustrate why it will be successful.

13.4 TALKING TO CLIENTS: THE PROJECT TEXT AND THE PRESS RELEASE

Architects, like any other specialised profession, use jargon. For example, they use the word 'volume' to describe three-dimensional form while us layfolk would think of this as a book or magazine or, quite rightly, the sound level of our car stereo. Some call this language 'archispeak'. What's really at fault here is a difference in exposure. Reaching back through many years of education, architects spend countless hours discussing ideas with peers, and have developed a specialised language that facilitates this. On the other hand, clients, stakeholders and users simply have not had this exposure. Some architects seem to take some pleasure in intimidating with intricate language, while other intellectual architects, like Rem Koolhaas, still manage to communicate ideas with a more accessible vocabulary. This is due, no doubt, to the fact that Rem Koolhaas used to be a journalist and can communicate complex ideas in a way that the public understands.

These heads of international practices effectively use language in their own way to support a unique persona. If the public does not understand it, this represents a missed communication opportunity. It is a missed opportunity to connect with and convince a client or the press. The journalist then becomes the 'archispeak' filter. They will ensure that they write in a style that is accessible to their readers, but how much translation work do we want to leave to journalists? Architects can learn from journalists and produce texts that are perhaps less cerebral self-reflection and more genuine communication.

The primary form of written communication for architects is project texts and press releases. Academic texts are not necessarily marketing, so I will not address them at this point. For both forms of written communication in question, it is essential that you ask yourself who your audience is. This is different for a new museum in a meadow outside the city than for a housing project in the inner city, which may be subject to public scrutiny.

The press release is a pragmatic text that adheres to certain rules. Make it look and sound like a newspaper article. The more successful you are at this, the more likely you are to succeed. I said this earlier but I have to say it again here: journalists are under constant time pressure. If you prepare your communication for a copy-and-paste job, you may stand out from the crowd, because the competition is fierce. In the Netherlands, for every journalist there are eight communication professionals. Often these journalists are freelancers juggling multiple contracts. Making their work easy could result in gaining an advantage over your competitors.

Project text is the purest explanation of the project. It is your design vision, in your words. You can do anything you like. However, if you take time to consider your audience, you will be more effective. If the project text is for peers, by all means use 'archispeak' and write to your peers as they would write to you. If the project faces political controversy, stakeholder consultation or is dependent on public participation, you would be wise to write it in a way that enables civilians to understand your vision. There is nothing stopping you from writing two versions of your project text and using different versions whenever needed.

WHAT CAN ARCHITECTS LEARN FROM SPEAKING TO CHILDREN?

If you have difficulty describing your project in clear language, use this simple trick: explain your project to an eight-year-old child. This challenge will cure you from using convoluted language. This level of explanation is incredibly useful and suitable for people without an architectural background. This is not arrogance, but rather clearly illustrates how far from regular language architectural jargon is. Non-architects often have decision-making power and heavily influence project development. For this reason, you may need to adapt your language not just in press releases and project text, but also in presentations.

Remember that you must strive for a fine balance. Using sophisticated vocabulary in your language to your client might communicate a high level of expertise, or it might be totally ineffective. I would suggest that you use the language of the client. For example, with a project developer who has a financial background, it would help the architect to better connect with the client by highlighting financial benefits in the design argument instead of emphasising luxurious and seemingly excessive design features. By doing so, the architect might convince the project developer that the project is perfect in financial terms. However, exactly this same language could alienate architectural peers.

PRACTICAL TIPS REGARDING THE PROJECT TEXT AND THE PRESS RELEASE

- **Test your language.** If you write a text, test it by asking someone who fits your target audience to read and comment.
- **Collaborate in text creation.** A chance to collaborate with the client, the user or the municipality on the press release is a great opportunity. Your reach will be that much greater. All stakeholders will have to agree on the communication, and this can be a challenging and sometimes emotional process ('I need more credits', etc.). At the end of the day, it marks the beginning of a great collective communication.
- **Follow established press release standards.** Look up online or in a book how to write the perfect press release. There are clear rules to follow which help to make a press release more effective. Some tips: include a powerful headline that draws attention. Include a lead (the bold section

at the start of a newspaper article) that summarises what the reader can expect. In the body text, answer the 'w' questions (what, where, when, why, who?). Prioritise information so that with the last paragraph cut off, it would still be a great article.

- **Use neutral language.** If you would like the text to be copy-and-pasted by journalists, ensure that it has an unbiased tone and avoid using praising adjectives in the description of your work. For example, instead of 'a beautiful glass front', you might write something more neutral but still positive, like 'a wide glass front allowing natural light to fall'.
- **Peers versus commercial clients.** Be aware that commercial clients love to speak and hear about the building's price tag, its efficient construction process, as well as its rental or sales potential. Peers who could be on the aesthetic committee or the competition jury have a different priority. Ensure that you respond to different groups using their own language and address their interests.

PATRIK SCHUMACHER, PARAMETRICISM MANIFESTO

'Contemporary avant-garde architecture is addressing the demand for an increased level of articulated complexity by means of retooling its methods on the basis of parametric design systems. The contemporary architectural style that has achieved pervasive hegemony within the contemporary architectural avant-garde can be best understood as a research programme based upon the parametric paradigm. We propose to call this style: Parametricism.'

Parametricism Manifesto
patrikschumacher.com, by Patrik Schumacher, London, 2008

13.5 THE MODEL

Models are perhaps the oldest and most traditional means for an architect to communicate spatial ideas to a client. They facilitate an understanding of the design on a much more playful and intuitive level (Figure 13.5.1). This is especially the case in participation processes, where models are great design tools if architects and clients (or stakeholders) manipulate and work on the models as part of the discussion.

As with all communication, a critical question is, 'Who is my audience?' I prefer artistic and abstract models that are real art pieces, and that illustrate the conceptual essence of a project rather than its detailed features. Use this communication medium with a discrete group of people, particularly those who enjoy and can appreciate the abstract side of architecture. I remember that when we sent a wonderfully abstract plaster model to a client, they asked why we did not include windows in the scheme. We followed up with a realistic model. An abstract model might not be useful for a school board on a tight budget, or a client who is new to architecture and apprehensive about the design process. The more realistic a model is, the more the public will understand it. So endeavour to make the model look attractive and be a good ambassador for your project. You would be wise to make the model abstract or sketchy if, for example, the design is not fully defined, or if it is a proposal that might be scrutinised by stakeholders of all sorts. Each detail and each balcony might invite critique, and divert attention from more important discussions.

Branding is also essential to your model. It is a product of your work so regard it as such, even if you commissioned an external model maker. It should reflect your company values. For example, if you are a practice specialising in wood, a plastic 3D printed model would not be cohesive with your brand. However, architects often face situations where a commercial client will make a realistic, and potentially less attractive, physical model of the project. This might be for a real estate fair or to display in their own lobby. If you can exercise some control and influence over its production, do. If not, don't worry. It may serve to communicate only with a niche group, and therefore not challenge your company branding.

Figure 13.5.1 *Guangzhou Opera House competition, MVRDV. The architecture model can have tactile qualities that are hard to reach with images.*

Using images of models to explain and present your project can be a powerful means of communicating your work and craft. There is a certain nostalgia in physical models particularly suited to specific communication efforts. For example, if you are a young firm that has not yet demonstrated the ability to realise a building, a physical model may serve as a more convincing medium than a render.

In addition to physical models, virtual reality or models in augmented reality are other mediums to explore. Public clients are especially pleased to walk through buildings to fully understand them before giving the green light for the construction. As the technology is in its infancy, often the aesthetic impression resembles the first computer-generated images from the 1990s, resulting in grey and dull buildings. If this is the case, ensure that clients also see the render, the collage or the physical model, in order to understand that the project is, in reality, compelling and attractive. Software progresses so quickly that it is only a matter of time before we have wonderful virtual buildings to walk through. Our children already have this in video games, so architecture will most assuredly follow suit.

PRACTICAL TIPS REGARDING MODELS

Engage nostalgia for physical models. For many people, physical models evoke fond childhood memories of playing with Lego and toy trains, and the nostalgia of toy-store vignettes. This encounter with a model will likely draw a smile from your guests as they peer into its toy-like scale. To facilitate this connection, you can display your models in your office. Ensure that your models are dust-free and well maintained. Dusty models in poor shape evoke negative feelings, and communicate that your architecture is redundant.

Make important parts of spatial use visible. If you design a store, you want to demonstrate that it will be a successful, profitable business. A very simple way of doing this is populating your model with shoppers carrying filled bags. Using humans in your models also provides a sense of scale, which is much more tangible than a legend.

Use the model as a design tool. When designing a home for private clients, or when involved in a public participation process, a physical model is a wonderful means of collaborating with the public to demonstrate, discuss and understand their needs and wishes.

Should you go with a 3D or a physical model? Both the physical model and the virtual 3D model have their own power. Remember that, for now, the physical model is easier to visit, that it gets an immediate response and that you do not require computers or additional technical staff to introduce it to larger crowds. A benefit is that parts of it can be shared online, or used in presentations. On the other hand, the virtual 3D model (at least at the present time) is a tool used to demonstrate your design to select clients and stakeholders. This is simply because only one or two people can tour the virtual model at a time. Not to mention the fact that it can be a hazard to personal pride: I can't tell you how many clients I've seen walk into walls wearing VR goggles.

CHAPTER 14
THE BUILT PROJECT

As far as marketing, PR and business development are concerned, a completed building is your best reference. With a completed building, you have physical evidence that you are able to realise a project, and you have a 'marketing folder' clients can visit in person. The three stages during which the building can play a marketing role are construction, opening and post-occupation.

CONSTRUCTION

Visiting a site with your potential clients and users presents a strong argument to engage them for future opportunities. The construction company is not usually keen to participate, but this kind of activity can potentially make or break the future success of the building. During the construction of Markthal Rotterdam, we invited more than 12,000 visitors to the site.[1] With each visitor cohort, we had different goals. First, we invited neighbours so they could understand the construction process. Next, we invited the public for days with specific themes, such as 'architecture day' or 'national construction day'. During these events, we toured the site with them, with the understanding that the public are the building's future users and potential clients. We also toured the site, as well as the model apartments, with potential buyers. Also, we invited potential business owners to a sales booth designed to resemble the Markthal in order to generate their interest in leasing space within it. Finally, we invited journalists to visit the site, to write about the building and to create a buzz even before it had opened. Hosting all of these different groups was most definitely a challenge for the construction company, but having learned from this success, we are determined to ensure that we can have this kind of access to a site during construction. This is so important that we include this access in our contracts. If necessary, we undertake security training to ensure the safety of visitors on site.

OPENING

A very common situation is just at the moment when the client and architect are in a tense situation, squabbling over final details like less expensive tiles or a delayed final payment, they also have to work together to organise an opening party. In large projects, the architect is often the smallest company involved, yet we must bear an equal responsibility with respect to the cost of organising opening festivities, or stand a chance of not having full access. At this point, you would be wise to exercise some diplomacy, in order to explain the value of the architect in the execution and promotion of the building. There are often important people at building openings, like politicians, investors and, in some cases, even royals. Assert yourself to ensure that you have a suitable role in the opening festivities and have an opportunity to make connections. Quite rightly, the developer may wish to be front and centre in leading the attending royal through the building, so it is up to you and your charismatic negotiating to land an influential role in the proceedings. Some flexibility and modesty might be required, but consider your ambition: a building opening is the beginning of a building's public life. It is the first step of its public reception and success, and if it is a prominent building for the local community, this is a prime press opportunity.

POST-OCCUPANCY

In short, it is important to remain involved in the building's operation and performance. For example, you may in future wish to tour it with potential clients. To this end, develop a solid relationship with the owner and occupants, as well as with the janitor and the staff in charge of keys, who can grant you access. You may have designed the building, but it is no longer in your control, so a considerable degree of courtesy is necessary to maintain a good relationship. I recall once that a group of architects walked into a rehearsal by Joe Cocker. The singer was furious, though I am not certain if this was because the hapless group interrupted his rehearsal, or because they focused on ceiling structure rather than his music. All that matters is that this little gaffe barred the architects from future entry. After occupation, remember that you are a guest in your own creation.

Your building is also a marketing tool and you should make every effort for it to look perfect. It is in your own interest that it evolves seamlessly. If, for example, you offer to help the owners and occupants with minor changes at no charge, they may consult you before applying the wrong sunscreens or out-of-tone street furniture. This is a win-win situation for both parties.

If you tour your building with potential clients or stakeholders, consider how this building relates to their potential building. Keep the general storyline of the building intact, yet short, and then discuss their ambitions. For example, a group of architects might want to hear more about the

Figure 14.1 *MVRDV client Ghislaine van de Kamp on the roof of her Didden Village project, Rotterdam. Satisfied clients are the best advertisement. Visiting your projects and having new clients talk to former clients can be a wonderful and informal way of persuasion.*

concept and see some smart details, while a group of civil servants might want to hear more about the building's ownership model. First, query the group about their preferences and combine your story with their ambitions. This can enhance the tour with the feeling that you went to the effort of customising it to their needs. I strongly suggest that part of the tour includes a meeting with a current occupant, or with the client who built it. Here again, it is a good idea to prepare them in advance, and ensure that they don't say something harmful to your reputation. They must understand the reason that you are visiting, and the ambitions you have for the tour. In terms of marketing effect, a happy occupant/owner is the best promotion you could hope to achieve (Figure 14.1).

PRACTICAL TIPS REGARDING THE BUILT PROJECT

Postpone the official construction-completion date. Your building will be a reference for future work, particularly in public tendering procedures. Public tenders often disqualify reference projects with completion dates beyond a five-year period, or at the very least, your reference project may receive fewer points if it is older than five years. To that end, it is useful to delay the official construction date until the very last piece of work is complete, and secure a letter from the client as evidence. In some countries, you can revise the completion date if you have done some changes to the building after it is in operation.

Monitor construction phases. In tenders, clients may sometimes want information about the duration of the phases of the construction. You might not remember this in three years' time, so ensure that you document this information clearly, especially any reasons for delay.

Develop strong connections with past clients. Stay in touch with the building, and its community, and learn from its performance. Users are often happy to share their insights, as well as suggestions for improvements. Users also appreciate contact with architects to share how pleased they are with the building. Occasionally, a new project comes from this contact. Just make sure you stay in touch, and maintain a direct line of contact with the occupant and client should they wish to reach you. Architects have an undeserved reputation for being arrogant. This is your opportunity to improve this reputation by listening, and learning from your experience to apply in your next commission, or possibly acquire another one.

Offer assistance when and where possible. When an ageing population in one of our buildings wanted a wind-screen in front of the main entrance, we designed it at no additional cost. Why? Because in doing this, we preserved the integrity of the design, and at the same time, inhabitants had a safer entrance. For us, it was important that the users were comfortable and that the screen that facilitated this comfort did not compromise the legibility of the main entrance.

CHAPTER 15
THE PROJECT BOOK

By now, you will understand the recurring theme of this book: the translation effort you must make in order to reach your clients, as this deviates from your core business. The project book is one of the key translation efforts.

For example, if a client pays £100,000, they pay for design services and not for a book. However, in many practices, the book is the only product the client can hold in his or her hands, and share with others. In terms of adhering to the core business of architecture, the most rational choice would be to simply print all the plans, bind them and present the project book to the client. Not so fast. Reading plans requires an architectural knowledge. Therefore, we must translate the plans and explain them with the help of texts, diagrams, reference images, renders or even watercolour paintings if needed.

This project book must be as strong as the design, and again the architect needs to be a *homo universalis*, able to design clear and legible diagrams, write compelling narratives and make a structured layout and storyline for this book. This is often the communication piece for your project. A good book explains to the client whether you can actually realise the building. It is an integral tool of persuasion and, as such, has the potential to go horribly wrong. The best building design ever, when represented poorly in a book, can still fail. What can go wrong, you ask? You can write too much or too little text, you can fail to include important information or you can fail to explain the project in a way that your client understands. In addition, the layout might be wrong for the project, and appear unprofessional. In the worst case, it can confuse the client and communicate the impression that you are not capable of building the project.

To prevent this, consider how you might explain the project to a client without standing next to them. In essence, the book should replace you. Though there are many exceptions, it is important for the first project book to answer basic questions your client may have:
- What is the design?
- How does it work?
- What will it cost?

- How do you build it?
- You might consider including information about strategies for building maintenance (cleaning, green technology, etc.).

A significant part of this challenge is answering all these questions within a great layout. First, the book design must represent the philosophy of your company. For example, at MVRDV we don't believe in too many additional distractions on pages, but some architects add navigation or page furniture on every page, while others include a small logo of the building as page decoration. Include whatever you believe will work for your client. You may impress some clients with pages upon pages of technical explanation and details, while other clients might be more interested in the visitor experience, the urban context or the price. When in doubt, consider what you would want to know from your architect if you were to build this project.

PRACTICAL TIPS REGARDING PROJECT BOOKS

Map out a storyline. Remember, the book takes the place of you explaining the project to your client in person. Think about whether your client will understand the concepts, and test it on someone who has never seen the project before. Does your test reader understand the project book? Is it clear what is so special about this particular design?

Diversify the depth of information. As in a magazine, you can create two tracks of information. Highlight key communication points in a short sentence above the main body of the text so that someone who just browses through the book still understands the essence of the project. For example, on a page with diagrams, as well as in the explanation of the construction, you could highlight a sentence such as, 'The project is comprised of wood construction and a concrete core.' This summarises essential information.

Exercise caution before you invest too heavily in competition books. These are a special print typology because they often have strict formatting constraints in terms of content and layout. Many architects think that a special binding or a luxury box will persuade the jury to think that the office is professional. I am not saying that it does not work like this, but more often than not, the competition assistant dismantles, scans and copies it. If this happens, the luxury binding has no purpose.

Participate in a jury. Have you ever been part of a jury that must decide between 10 outstanding projects? If not, do, and you can discover how to make a good book. Instead of reading lengthy texts, jury members tend to browse through massive amounts of information, capturing only details that are clearly pronounced. The easier you make it for the jury to find the right information, the more likely they will read it and digest it. A clear and understandable competition book gives you an advantage over your competitors.

CHAPTER 16
EXHIBITIONS

Architecture and urban planning are complex, so, in turn, architecture and urbanism exhibitions are complex. With the desire to impress peers, we collect mountains of information, photographs, diagrams and long-winded written explanations for exhibitions. The resulting piece's abundance of information makes it impossible to digest in a single visit. This hardly fulfils the objectives for exhibiting in the first place.

Consider the typical visitor at the Venice Architecture Biennale. There are around 60 pavilions with an exhibition, countless room-side exhibitions in the Italian pavilion and the Arsenale, and there are side events all over the city. The typical visitor stays two or three days, far too little time to read everything on display. How much of the abundant displays do they digest fully? It is no wonder that the Golden Lion for best exhibition once went to a café. The place was far more expert at capturing visitor attention than lengthy textual analysis.

Exhibiting architecture is no easy task. The work of Peter Eisenman in a clear-white-box environment with 'archispeak' texts needs far more time than a manga-cartoon-style exhibition by hip practice BIG. However, there is so little time in Venice, and so much to see. After digesting so many exhibitions, which ones will you remember? The cool South American bar where you had a beer or the intellectual depth of a deconstructivist masterpiece?

Again, it boils down to communication. Exhibition architecture is a discrete discipline, but with some general parameters, you can be effective. This starts by evaluating the nature of the event, the interests of the visitors and the approximate time they will spend with your exhibition. When you're planning, ask interrogative questions: who, why, what and when are you exhibiting? If you think that your average visitor has not paid an entrance fee, is not an architect and has but five minutes for your exhibition, you need to design something very different from designing for an audience of peers who may spend up to 20 minutes with your display, and have paid an entrance fee. Whom you design for is a fundamental question you must solve before you sit at the drawing board.

Figure 16.1 *The Serpentine Pavilion, by MVRDV, 2004. It was the only pavilion that was not realised, being plagued by cost issues and incomplete sponsorships. Budgets are often an issue with exhibitions.*

The annual Serpentine Pavilion (Figure 16.1), realised in Hyde Park, London, is a wonderful example of an exhibition that allows the public to experience architecture. Its intelligence lies in events in the space, but visitors of all backgrounds can equally enjoy the physical experience. The Architektur Galerie Berlin has also transformed to become an experience-based exhibition, limiting lengthy texts and screens.

At the other end of the scale is the International Architecture Biennale Rotterdam. This is totally peer centred and often exhibits urbanism, which is even more complex than architecture. Here, the exhibition is unapologetic about its dense content, rendering it really only digestible for the profession, and even peers are not always able to digest all the content.

Often the biggest impact an exhibition makes occurs during its first two days. During the opening, VIPs and the press visit, and they define how the public receives your exhibit. They also come to network and enjoy a few drinks, so the parameters for the first days are different. Keep this in mind when designing. If you have the chance to attend, and be an ambassador for your exhibition, it will be to your advantage.

For project presentations in a city, other rules apply. Municipal clients often want to promote their new project to citizens in order to gain public approval, so entering a discussion about long texts and abstract models may challenge this objective.

In general, we might say that an exhibition is again a translation of your work to the public, and here the parameters have changed to include the demographics and physical behaviour of your visitors. You are designing a physical visitor experience, which ideally goes beyond being a magazine on wallpaper.

PRACTICAL TIPS REGARDING EXHIBITIONS

Consider what your objective is. It's very important to keep in mind what you want to achieve with this exhibition. Do you need public approval for a building? Do you want your peers to get a sense of your intellect? Do you want to show how innovative you are? Each case demands a different approach.

Be brief. You know personally that it is not comfortable to read a long text while standing. Either keep it short or position chairs facing it, should you think you need to explain it in depth.

Prepare handouts. If your audience has little time or is overwhelmed with other exhibitions in the same venue, why not prepare a handout (or better, QR code) that allows the audience to read your texts and view your detailed plans on their own time?

Make it tactile. An exhibition is a real space that allows people to interact, touch and feel. Rather than just presenting a render of a brick façade and asking your audience to look at it, perhaps also combine it with real samples of brick, so they can touch and feel. It becomes a more accessible and tactile experience.

Make it local. Your audience might be more interested when the show is somehow locally relevant. If you can, it might be a great way to connect better with the locals.

Keep your target group in mind. Who you design the show for defines the design. Design everything with your audience and their expectations in mind.

Keep time limits in mind. How much time does your audience have, and can they read and digest your message in that given time?

- **Make connections with tours.** If the venue provides tour guides, rehearse with them. The tour guides might become much better if they tell your story – try to help them.
- **Stay present during the opening.** During the opening, there will be VIPs and press around so try to stay near your display and explain it to anyone interested. There are plenty of drinks during openings. Depending on the potential for the future of your business, moderate your intake in order to present your business professionally. Remember that this is work, even though it feels like a party.

CHAPTER 17
PRIORITISING

How much PR can a single person do? If you would like to execute all of the advice I've explained in the preceding chapters, you will require more than one full-time PR person in your practice. As a start-up or small firm, you likely do not have the luxury.

How do you prioritise? First, create a professional aura around your company. This includes an office interior that resonates with your design philosophy, your vision and mission, as well as a website and corporate identity that accomplish this. The real PR work should be in relation to the time you have, but remember, it is very efficient to publicise in press or social media because the more coverage you receive, the more people will discover you, and hire you. To this end, I would advise you to establish a consistent public presence.

Prioritise the things you do easily. You may enjoy being active on Instagram, for example, or find it easier to attend industry events, lectures and networking opportunities. You may wish to focus on public speaking at events in which you can meet potential clients.

If you have very little time to apply to PR, it is best to focus on events with the highest return on investment. In order to arrive at the right decision in terms of efficiency, you can ask the liberating question, 'What would happen if I just ignore this?' If the answer is, 'It won't really impact my future,' maybe this event is not the right one. However, in my experience, new projects lie around unexpected corners, so I view every event with a glass-is-half-full perspective. That said, this is my job, whereas PR work may be only one of a complex and daunting number of tasks that are part of your role as an architect-entrepreneur. Your time is precious, so use it in the best way, but don't forget the credo, 'If I was down to my last dollar, I would spend it on public relations' (see Chapter 7).

PR is important: just do it.

PRACTICAL TIPS REGARDING SETTING PRIORITIES

Follow your talent. Define what lies closest to your own interest. Work on that part yourself and find ways to prioritise and outsource the rest.

Hire a PR agency. If you cannot afford to invest any time in PR, or you find it loathsome and want to spend your time differently, you could try to hire a PR agent. If you do this, it is important to discuss clear goals and market perspective. PR is not an exact science, and the PR agency may not want to adhere to clear goals, but managing expectations is important. They will ask for a monthly fee as part of this. To support this, you should draft a common goal that serves to articulate ambitions in terms of publications, as well as measurable impact, with weekly meetings and a monthly overview of the work they performed.

Make a fun PR package. Investigate all the potential ways you can do PR and choose the work that you like to do. Enthusiasm makes the task easier.

Divide and conquer. Divide the work between you and your business partner (should you have one), but be aware that PR work can have a bad influence on the dynamics within a practice. If only one of the partners dominates in the media, the world might form the mistaken impression that he or she is the principal. If the other principals support this, this is fine, but I would suggest that you do media appearances together or attempt to maintain a balance. Alternatively, agree on what your relative strengths are and work accordingly. You may be better at approaching new clients, whereas your partner may enjoy attending fairs or other business events.

CHAPTER 18
BUSINESS DEVELOPMENT, THE DIRECT WAY TO WIN NEW WORK

So far in this book, I have established what I believe effective public relations to be, and emphasised that PR can be open-ended and unpredictable. It deals with press and publications, and involves a concerted effort to create your and your company's reputation. This open-ended effort may or may not attract new business. Often the more direct approach to winning new work is through business development.

The moment you launch a company, you are an entrepreneur. The moment you convince your first client to select you, you are a business developer for your company. Was it only a quaint conversation and then it evolved naturally into a commission? Yes, that, too, is business development.

The most direct approach to business development you can take is to call a potential client, secure a meeting, present yourself and your work, and thereafter receive a project. Many firms I queried have a principal who actively meets clients, sometimes over drinks, and these personal relationships invariably evolve into project commissions. London-based architect Phil Coffey (see Case Study 4) refers to this activity as 'going out there, losing my liver'. A less liver-taxing way to network is in meetings at fairs, conferences or other events that allow unsolicited approaches and facilitate face time with a potential client.

Another means of obtaining new business is responding to public or commercial tenders, and receiving the award of the work through an arduous public procedure. There is a multitude of commercial tender websites that sell subscriptions to public tender feeds. For example, in the European Union there is the EU TED website, there is Tenderstream for public tenders all over the world, and in the UK there are different regional procurement websites. What they all have in common is mediated contact with the client through the procurement advisor. Therefore, the business case becomes reference and data-driven, making your chances slimmer unless you have a specialised portfolio.

Direct commissions are wonderful, and come about through the reputation you establish. Clients may come across your work and contact you directly, or perhaps they do this after some PR work you have done. Studio MUTT (see Case Study 3) noticed how this works after one of their projects went viral on social media. There is also a potential downside to these direct commissions: you don't really have an opportunity to be selective if you're reliant on these kinds of commissions. If a client offers you a project, it's difficult to say, 'No, in my business plan I did not include a commercial office project.' It may happen that you find yourself building a portfolio in an area you had not anticipated and may not enjoy.

Creating your own projects is another option that some architects manage successfully. For example, Turner Works (see Case Study 7) have specialised in finding spaces to transform temporarily or permanently, the value of which others might not have recognised. These architects are able to identify opportunities and build a multidisciplinary team around them to mobilise projects.

Some practices specialise in just one means of BD, while others attempt all possibilities in order to distribute risk. There is also a difference with respect to typologies: large public building projects aren't really acquired over a conversation in the pub, but you might be successful with this kind of networking for more commercial projects.

CHAPTER 19
CLIENT RELATIONSHIPS:
A PERSONAL 'CLICK' OR A FINANCIAL AGREEMENT?

The old adage that we are hard-wired to make a judgement in the first few seconds of meeting someone rings true in the world of project acquisition as well. In addition to factual considerations such as your portfolio, awards and other design achievements, the decision to hire you for a commission also involves a human factor. Although somewhat immeasurable, this might be more impactful than we imagine.

A construction project is a long and involving process. Entering into this kind of relationship means that you and your potential client will meet each other regularly, possibly for the next three to ten years. It's no surprise that the decision becomes personal. Clients might want to work with an architect they can sit down and have a pint with (though this may never actually happen). If they can imagine that, you're more likely to get the job. Keep in mind that at these initial evaluation meetings, you are not just presenting your work, you are also presenting yourself as a partner for this project.

For private residences, the personal 'click' is particularly important. Designing a home is an intimate process in which the couple might reveal that they have separate bedrooms, or that they refuse to share a toilet. You will be privy to more intimate information than even some friends or family.

Personal relationships influence large projects as well. Imagine you win a competition. The first phase is euphoric, then you start to define the design and budget cuts creep in and strain the relationship. Or, during construction, the client might make decisions that you do not agree with which leads to tension in front of contractors. I have often experienced that during the last leg of the construction project, when PR is busy organising the opening, the relationship between architect and client is at its lowest point. The reason for this is often a disagreement over finishing details such as tiles or the colour of walls.

Like all relationships, the relationship with your client requires maintenance. As you are the service provider, you must maintain it. This is especially true for architects because they rarely adhere to the mantra 'the customer is always right'.

Figure 19.1 *Client relationships need to be authentic. If your clients invite you to a port-themed party in Rotterdam, it's perhaps best to accept only if you really fancy it. Business Developer Daan van Gool (centre) with clients celebrating his birthday.*

Becoming friends with clients can be incredibly effective in two ways: you forgive each other more easily if there are problems during the process and you might get more than one project out of the client.

These friendships come in different variations, just like in real life. With some clients there is a close relationship where you might attend concerts together; you meet their spouse; you know the names of each other's kids. This kind of friendship is authentic (Figure 19.1): you should not attempt to fake this because it will be obvious.

Then there is the formalised friendship in which you invite each other for social but more formal gatherings, mostly networking, such as a sailing trip or a golf day.

And there are the polite friendships in which you invite the client to dinner or lunch and they return the favour. This is especially important when you have foreign clients who visit you, who won't necessarily have evening entertainment planned.

The most technocratic relationships develop within larger projects, where big teams of consultants and architects meet an equally big developer's team. Even here everybody is human. Your behaviour during these meetings can be crucial. Are you friendly, flexible, smart and listening? Do you acknowledge others and do you behave in a way that means others might want to work with you again?

There are certainly architects who behave as if they are geniuses who are not bothered with normal relationships, but you need to be high in the pecking order to behave like this. In general, it's wise in personal relationships to be likable, friendly and flexible. This doesn't mean that you have to give up your philosophy. On the contrary, a great personal relationship with a client might make it easier in the course of the project to defend some of your choices.

PRACTICAL TIPS REGARDING CLIENT RELATIONSHIPS

Balance. There is a balance regarding what degree of personal weight a professional relationship can handle; maintaining these relationships requires some tact and empathy.

Be nice. It's not rocket science: if the client likes you, they will potentially grant you more work.

Be careful. It may look like a friendship, but it's also a client/service-provider relationship and you need to be careful about revealing anything that might trouble this relationship. This does not mean that you cannot be authentic and discuss learning curves – that is certainly an added value to a closer relationship with a client.

Confidentiality. Be careful with confidential information. Never share information about your other clients or projects that should not be shared.

Cultural differences. It's advisable to discuss business culture before you venture abroad. Many Chinese clients, for example, put a value on getting drunk together because it shows your real character; a test and a bonding moment. In France, there is a moment to discuss business, and it's not during a dinner. In Scandinavia, they run out of meetings at 4:30pm, even though there might be a terrible crisis in the project, because private life is considered equally important. Some preparation will help you to overcome awkward moments. Should you cause offence by accident, just acknowledge it and explain that you did not mean any harm. In the US, I had to explain to a client who confronted us with a sad story why we didn't cry, like other architects: 'We are just as upset as the others, but Europeans rarely cry in public.'

Introverted characters. If you, for example, have trouble with small talk, you can take classes in how to do this. But it's also possible for some introverted characters to be contagiously enthusiastic about their own work, and this can make a great impression during a first meeting.

Classes. If you notice that you experience some problems with client relationships, you could take classes or training to overcome the problem, such as how to pitch or how to be more assertive to achieve your goals, or even how to do small talk.

CHAPTER 20
WHO IS YOUR CLIENT AND HOW DO YOU APPROACH THEM?

In order to better serve the character and needs of their customers, and ultimately sell more, marketing professionals first define their target-group profiles. This is the reason that Currys PC World uses a red colour in its marketing, and that Holland & Barrett pervasively uses the colour green. The colour red attracts dominant individuals in search of a good deal for a new gadget, while the colour green assures those in search of security, natural health and beauty items that all products are anointed by Mother Nature herself (Figure 20.1). This is due to subliminal messaging which communicates with the emotional, limbic centre of the brain, accounting for the vast majority of an individual's decisions. Even if you spend months on end evaluating different vehicles, your brain's emotional centre may have already made the decision, your well-intended research done in vain. Your critical faculties then actively support the emotional decision as a rational one.

Given the risk involved in large real estate projects, rational decision-making holds court, but the architect's selection can potentially be emotional. With this in mind, there is huge scope to apply a marketing perspective to the competitive process.

Think about who you are as an individual, and who your client might be.

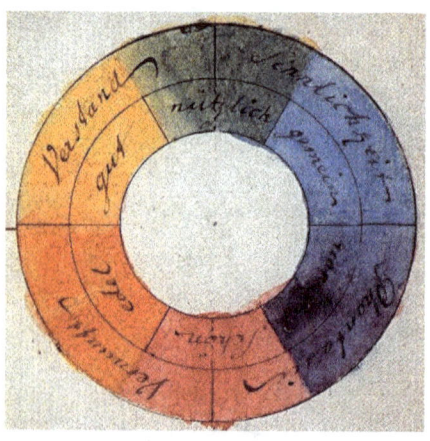

Figure 20.1 The colour circle by Goethe (1810), which is used today in marketing, adds psychology to colours. The colours of the cover of this book communicate trustworthiness and rationality.

There are all kinds of personality tests online, which might indicate what kind of sales person you are. Many of these divide personality types into four different profiles: dominant, innovative, social and security-driven. Architects are more often than not innovation-driven, and real estate clients are business-oriented, dominant and competitive. This means that architects interested in content and innovation must convince a person driven by wanting to be the best, or wanting to achieve significant ambitions. If you know this, you can pitch in line with how your client thinks. Perhaps a dominant client wants to hear about the awards your projects have won or profits your former clients have amassed due to your innovative design work. Perhaps they might be interested in how the project achieved a sought-after standard, and how working with you can help their project achieve it too.

It's not always that black and white, and there are certainly many conflicting issues and grey zones. A dominant client might be looking for a socially driven architect because their particular project needs this, and the client cannot achieve this alone. Speaking your client's language and addressing their unique needs in your sales approach is an integral part of a strong strategy.

You might not always be able to analyse the client beforehand, but a simple Google search and a tour of their website is a solid foundation. Do this before you meet them, as they will know when you haven't done your due diligence. Demonstrate interest in them, and enquire about the highlights in their portfolio; mention projects of theirs that you admire. Flexibility is also a great virtue. I was once in a meeting with a potential commercial development firm client. The director lamented how conceptual architects are not able to design details. I abruptly diverted from the presentation I had prepared, and instead showed a small store we had designed which illustrated an amazing innovation in detailing. The director appreciated this, but sadly, we did not receive a follow-up. A year later, I met him at a real estate fair and prepared a short but assertive presentation that showed construction methods and square-foot prices of our projects, while normally we would discuss the conceptual side of our architecture. Essentially, I said, 'Look, we grew up and we are ready to work for you.' Today, we work for this individual and I am very proud that we developed our skills to demonstrate a capacity for commercial architecture. This client recognised a skill deficit, and appreciated our ability to address it.

For public clients, you might want to illustrate a different side of your projects: perhaps the public impact your project has had. Adjusting how you discuss and present your project can be quite effective. During a presentation to a construction company, you want to discuss the smart construction. In a pitch to a developer, you may wish to discuss your financial approach and sales outcome. Different facets of your project can speak to different target groups. Try to analyse what your client's interests are and address these by evaluating your portfolio from their perspective.

Again, this is largely a translation effort. How do you speak to your client in order to convince them that you are the best architect to work with? You need not be apprehensive about diluting your design ethos: this is best suited for an audience of peers, where you discuss the passion you have for the project, and you don't mention budget details.

PRACTICAL TIPS REGARDING SALES APPROACH

Prepare. Preparation is integral to a successful sales conversation. This is not rocket science, so if a client builds commercial buildings, you might want to show your commercial projects. However, do take time to introduce your 'best of', just to show the breadth of your firm's skills. If you can, discuss the contents of the meeting beforehand with individuals involved so that you understand what interests them and you're not reliant entirely on Google searches.

Analyse. Try to predict their interests and prepare your presentation accordingly. Translate your portfolio so that it suits your potential client's interests.

Be flexible. If you prepare for showing your office portfolio, and – surprise – the potential client tells you during the meeting that they are now venturing into collective housing, be prepared to change everything on the spot.

Outsource. If you absolutely hate sales, there are companies that specialise in doing acquisition for you, and they offer full services, including preparing tender documents, as well as your financial offer. This can really enhance opportunities for a growing practice.

Enlist an agent. It is also sometimes handy to have an agent on board, who works with a commission of between 2 and 10% of your fee. The agent should put this percentage on top of the fee, so your client essentially pays for the agent's services.

CHAPTER 21
JUST DO IT

Speaking to many architects over the last few years, I often sense a certain hesitation towards proactive business development. They offer their introversion, or fear and confusion as to how to go about it, as reasons for inaction. This is all understandable, as most university studies develop architects' technical and conceptual skills but there is little attention paid to the business side of things. This is a significant omission because in starting their own studios, many architects become entrepreneurs.

To these dear friends and colleagues I usually say, 'Just do it.' This is often followed by, 'What's the worst thing that can happen?' It's important to strategise and prepare for every move you make, but contemplation should not become so daunting that this prevents you from taking the necessary steps because you're afraid you'll make a mistake. You are an entrepreneur, and this involves taking risks and bold steps to go further. You might meet 10 people who decline to hire you, but perhaps number 11 will. There is great virtue in developing a resolve. First, refine and refine your pitch. Second, build your network. Even if a potential client you meet is not for you, they may refer you to others who are. If it does not work the first time, try a year later, and again a year later. Eventually, your efforts will result in success. It's also important, even if you have the feeling after a few minutes that the meeting is pointless, to pursue. At the beginning of their career, the rock group Kiss often performed in front of small audiences, putting on the same wild shows they were eventually known for. They played small pubs as if they were Wembley, each time in full make-up.

The same logic applies to tenders. You may very well bomb procurement inboxes with your tender documents without any success in the beginning. However, you'll gain useful insights from this experience and develop a network of consultants and potential partners for future projects. When I started out in business development in 2008, at the beginning of the global financial crisis, I took on almost any tender I could lay my hands on. The success rate in these early days was a hopeful 1 in 20. We dreamed about increasing the probability to 1 in 10, and reached this goal three years later. Today, the success rate is much better; this is, in part, because we've learned to be much more critical in the evaluation process, analysing the tender carefully in terms of chances to win.

Figure 21.1 *A photorealistic render of the Netherlands Pavilion at Expo 2020 Dubai (postponed to 2021). V8 Architects from Rotterdam were able to secure the project based on some daring entrepreneurship.*

Another example I want to share is about a young architecture practice based in Rotterdam, called V8 Architects, that was approached by a developer. At the time, the developer was working with another architect to design a 150m residential tower – but the project did not go smoothly. The young architects were asked to design a so-called 'plan B'. The young architects thought about it, decided to take on the project, set up a bigger organisation and in the course of the project their design passed the city's 'beauty commission' instantly. The tower is under construction as we speak. This project kick-started a growth in their practice and today they are a mid-size practice with a wonderful portfolio, which also includes the design of the Netherlands Pavilion for the upcoming World Expo in Dubai (Figure 21.1). If they had worried too much about their small practice not being equipped for a project this size, they would not have grown so quickly. Sometimes taking a risk is worth it.

My aim here is to light a fire under you and to say that the first steps are the most difficult, but just starting will get you somewhere. This is not a straight line, but eventually you will succeed.

PRACTICAL TIPS REGARDING APPLYING A PROACTIVE APPROACH

Just do it! Try, experiment, make mistakes, learn from them, but get out there and fight for a seat at the table.

Be flexible. Take on the attitude of water in a stream: it does not matter whether the water passes the stone in the stream on the left or right side, as long as it flows.

CHAPTER 22
GOING ABROAD

While doing research for this book, and discussing business practices with UK architects, I asked them whether they would like to work abroad. Surprisingly, their answer was often no. They expressed numerous worries about the risks and bemoaned the fact that they speak no foreign languages.

This is a strange trepidation, because working globally is integral to de-risking the business of architecture in the small and sometimes volatile Dutch market, which routinely collapses for all kinds of reasons. For example, in 2020, all Dutch construction came to a halt simply because the air quality in nature reserves was poor. Many Dutch architects work abroad to sustain a more stable business. This is a Dutch tradition (Figure 22.1).

Sometimes these adventures to win work abroad fail, but the trip is rewarding. In spite of all the odds, often they result in new work. This is especially true if offer and demand match. When this happens, architects suddenly find they have become an internationally operating architecture firm, such as the then young architects Information Based Architecture and their whopping 462m Canton TV Tower in Guangzhou, China, completed in 2010.

Reluctance to go abroad has not always been the case. During the previous financial crisis of 2008, many UK architects went to the Emirates and thereafter established a British-style tender system. This formed the foundation for the structured development of Dubai and Abu Dhabi. The Brits often don't speak the language, but it still works. At MVRDV, it's the same. We don't speak all the languages of the 45 countries we work in, but we try to hire staff from the countries we work in and we do all speak some kind of English, the current lingua franca. Might there still be ambition and gut for the post-Brexit nation to go global?

MVRDV took 10 years to mature and then expand internationally. This is not a bad tactic because you learn to be a good architect, and then you learn to become an international architect. Nevertheless, if you're less established, but you have the ambition, by all means go for it. Architecture is incredibly translatable. There may be a different building code in every country, but these are only parameters: the fundamentals are the same. The core business

Figure 22.1 *The King and Queen of the Netherlands often combine a state visit with a trade mission. Here they are on a visit to Germany in 2013, accompanied by representatives from more than 100 companies.*

– designing great buildings and urban plans – is the same everywhere. Architecture might be a poorly paid position compared to others, but one of its benefits is the fact that it travels well. This can both enrich experience, as well as your expertise and portfolio.

A general rule of thumb is that you should have an objective when working internationally. If you are an expert of some sort, it makes sense to apply this expertise internationally. For example, Dutch architects Benthem Crouwel have built all the major train stations in the Netherlands over the past 20 years, to considerable public acclaim. It would follow that they export this expertise internationally.

If you endeavour to export your architectural expertise to foreign countries, make sure you are clear on what your unique value is, especially in comparison with what clients may get from a local architect. Perhaps you are a sustainable practice and you bring an innovative perspective to a country that is not as advanced? Perhaps you have a very strong signature architecture that is ready for export. If we look at the work of Zaha Hadid Architects, this is a clear and unique selling point. Even if you develop on less exportable architecture, say designs generated through the bespoke processes of public participation, you can still be attractive to an international market. This might be because you bring unique expertise to the process of design or perhaps as a foreigner you bring the unbiased perspective and expertise desperately needed to make necessary change. In many countries, there is an open spirit towards foreign experts. This philosophy stems from the belief (for better or for worse) that when it comes from abroad, it must be good.

How do you choose a country to work in? In an ideal situation, the country makes the choice for you because you have done some international PR and clients know how to find you. If this is not the case, analyse your strengths and try to determine countries in which this is missing. A basic but worthwhile tactic is to select your favourite holiday destination. I do this sometimes, because I love being in exciting new places, so it's an extra incentive for me to work harder and visit more often. This has brought us projects in Munich, Scotland, Taiwan and Israel.

To be successful, you must be a bit adventurous, entrepreneurial and view the world from an optimist's perspective. Although working abroad can be

Figure 22.2 *Tainan Spring, Tainan, Taiwan, MVRDV, 2020. More than 395 years after the Dutch built a fortress in Tainan, the MVRDV project Tainan Spring is a non-violent addition to the city.*

difficult, it also offers a great opportunity to enrich your practice and life. Whenever faced with the many problematic variables involved in working in a foreign country, I reflect on a special Dutch consolation. I once visited a Dutch fortress in Tainan, Taiwan (a city where MVRDV have recently completed a project, Figure 22.2). People travelled there and built this fortress on a sand bank (aided by slave labour, let's be honest, they were no sweethearts). They faced enormous risk. They travelled to the other side of the world in search of spices, unsure whether or not they would ever return, and with odds more in favour of failure and death than success. Still, they did it. Compared to these kinds of international exploits, working abroad in architecture is not so bad.

You would do well not to be too naïve, and to do your research. There are issues with finances, insurance, contracts and – yes – language. If you see these as great impediments, you might not want to take the risk. However, you can work through these, and do keep in mind that making a few mistakes is part of being an entrepreneur. There are glorious stories of failure, architects secreted out of a country under the cloak of night because they feared that an authoritarian government would arrest them. There are other stories of architects fleeing Moscow with suitcases full of cash. On the other hand, consider that architects have also designed highly acclaimed buildings in lands that were foreign to them, including the Guggenheim Bilbao, the Shard and the MoMA extension. You see, there can also be glorious successes.

Go for it. It's fun. Enjoy the surprised look on your client's face as they appraise your gifts of Marmite and Yorkshire Tea.

PRACTICAL TIPS REGARDING GOING ABROAD

Partners. If you are a full-service provider in the UK, you might not be one abroad. In many countries, foreigners do not have licences to practise as architects, so you need a trustworthy local partner. These partners must provide you with the knowledge about the local building code, and they should have a suitable portfolio of built projects. It goes without saying that you will need to work together under potentially trying circumstances, so make sure you have that 'click'. In terms of contracts: make sure that the position of your local partner towards yourself and the client is clear and that it represents the responsibilities in the right way.

Construction details. In many foreign countries, the construction drawings, tender documentation and the building permit are in the hands of your local partner. Choose well. The success of your project is in their hands, as the legal representative of your partnership.

Fee. The UK is one of the higher-earning countries in terms of architects' salaries, and this presents a slight disadvantage when working in the wider world. You might not be able to compete on fee, as mentioned above, so your unique selling point must be clear. What do you bring that a local firm does not bring? Don't overestimate this. It's often sufficient to be a foreign architect to have leverage in the selection process. Spanish magazine *Metalocus* once created a great infographic illustrating a comparison of different fees due to salaries. There are seven countries (in ascending order) which offer highest average monthly architecture salaries: Ireland ($4,651), Qatar ($4,665), Canada ($4,745), Australia ($4,750), United States ($5,918), UK ($6,146) and Switzerland ($7,374).[1]

Contracts. If you cannot push through your standard contract or the RIBA contract, attempt to negotiate all the important clauses into the contract. During the negotiations, it helps to ask why the contract includes certain clauses, rather than declining them outright. In many foreign countries, the architectural discipline is a protected discipline and there are legal arrangements. In Denmark, for example, the fact that a client pays you is enough evidence to apply architectural law, which protects you significantly (even if you have no signed contract). However, other countries are like the Wild West. When in doubt, ask your embassy, obtain a local lawyer or ask your partner architect.

Portfolio-building. Other countries have their own tender regulations, so perhaps you can secure your dream typology in China, even if you don't have the right references at home in Britain.

Cultural differences. They are real and they can be challenging, but with a little effort, they usually solve themselves. Then, there are legal concerns. In Thailand, you need to establish a Thai office to be an architect. In France, you need to pay an enormous amount of insurance (but the architect's fee is good) and in many places you can only call yourself a design consultant, even though the clients still appreciate seeing your architecture licence. In spite of all of this, the challenges of working abroad can be overcome, and practising architecture internationally is feasible.

Staff. An ambitious Italian architect once made a legendary mistake designing a social housing project in Holland. With all his ideals, and perhaps a bit of prejudice, he designed balconies larger than living rooms, without fully comprehending the sheer miserable extent of Dutch weather. You may design a typical Indian apartment, or typical Norwegian cladding with the help of your co-architect, but if the project is large enough, hire some local staff as they will make communication easier and ultimately prevent you from gaffes such as designing oversized balconies. Keep in mind that the local staff in your office might think it's disrespectful to tell you that you made a bad design decision, so ensure that you establish a receptive climate for conversation and design discussion.

Security. As Iraq was recovering from the Gulf War, MVRDV received an invitation to work in Erbil, a Kurdish city experiencing an oil boom. We declined because we felt it was not safe. In retrospect, this was a wise decision. When working internationally, don't send your staff to unsafe places, or to places that don't allow them to be who they are. For example, in some countries women and members of the LGBTQ+ community are not always safe. (See also Chapter 33, on ethics.)

CHAPTER 23
FAIRS

Once a year, the world of commercial real estate meets at MIPIM in Cannes. Here, attendees trade architecture and present investment opportunities. In terms of return, the countless building models on show are slick and company logos dominate.

Aside from MIPIM, there is MIPIM UK, Expo Real, Provada, Polis Convention, Cityscapes, BoDW and many more (Figures 23.1 and 23.2). There are also many local fairs in several British cities. As much as I loathe the general impression of trade fairs (it might surprise you, but I did not sign up to drift around a trade fair floor in a suit with a sponsored name badge around my neck, chatting to people who work for 'Invest Transylvania'), I have to admit they can be amazingly efficient. The people you encounter are engaging and focused, as the chats are short and, in my experience, often evolve into real projects. Their value is too great to ignore.

If you walk around a real estate fair for the first time, don't expect a great deal. Have a look, connect to your region's or city's stand, and see if they have some refreshments. If they do, casually chat to people and talk spontaneously. It's already a clear sign of your committed professionalism if you have made it this far, communicating that you have ambitions.

To apply more strategy to the endeavour, buy the ticket in advance (often this comes with a reduction), evaluate the participants list and contact the individuals you wish to speak to in advance. Be aware that you are probably on the bottom of the priority list, so it's smart to propose a date for one of the last days of the fair, as the important, pressing business transactions occur on the first and second day. Towards the end of the fair, potential clients have a little more time for you to try to sell them some architecture. Make an impactful and very commercial presentation. Think about what your potential client wants to see first: the type, surface area and budget, obviously. They do appreciate hearing about a project's profit and how quickly it was rented or sold.

I would also advise you to look for events at trade stands that allow you to chat with people who, for whatever reason, don't normally make appointments. I was able to connect with some mayors and ministers

Figure 23.1 *A busy Munich metro station, Messestadt West, during Expo Real, 2019.*

Figure 23.2 *Invest Glasgow stand during Expo Real, in Munich, 2017; the millions of visitors probably came in after the picture was taken...*

spontaneously, and this kind of impromptu connection can prove enormously useful; instead of pitching for a new project in this context, you can perhaps lobby for your upcoming project.

If you have an opportunity to be on the main stage of the event, you're likely a 'starchitect' of some kind, but occasionally organisers will invite lesser-known architects who have relevant innovation to share, or perhaps an intelligent way to reduce costs. Talking in front of a hall filled with potential clients is complete and utter PR bliss. Bar none, it is the best possible lecture in terms of acquisition, so carefully consider your presentation, and ensure that it does not become too obvious as a sales pitch. You want to ensure that relevant audience members contact you.

Having your own stand is an investment, but some larger architecture practices make the effort. This provides visibility, as well as a very professional presentation. The Dutch sister organisation of the RIBA has a stand every year at both MIPIM and Expo Real, which is very successful. We've been once at MIPIM with our own stand, which, with a large group of architects, was cheaper than buying individual tickets for all attendees. The downside is that you need to have someone at the stand at all times, so you can't just go out there and mingle. If you want to do that also, you need to send multiple attendees.

PRACTICAL TIPS REGARDING FAIRS

Price. Going to a fair is usually very expensive, so think about whether this is worth the investment and its return. If it's your first fair, keep your expectations low. You will need to attend a few times before you can navigate effectively and see a return. For new staff, we often buy a single day ticket and then multiple days for the next trade fair, to allow them time to acclimatise and reflect.

Filter. The investment is considerable so it's often only the boss who goes. This allows you to meet the potential client, the mayor or the head of urban planning, without their filters: the resolute secretary of the assistant. This is your opportunity to meet decision-makers, unencumbered. Just confirm whether they are open to small talk.

Plan ahead. If you want to make sure that you see a return on the investment of the entrance fee, make a few appointments well in advance. Don't be irritated if these meetings are not successful, or if they move your appointment around. Because you're trying to sell them something, you are treated as a sales person, and if they do agree to meet you, you should be pleased that they have agreed to reserve some of their incredibly expensive time at the fair for you.

Dress strategically. MIPIM, for example, is a black-suit world, and if you insist on wearing jeans, be prepared to be the only one. It's up to you to decide whether this is a good choice. If you want to stand out, why not?

Stand out. Companies which reserve a stand often stay for three full days, with meeting after meeting, and in the evenings they have network dinners and network drinks. How do you stand out in this cacophony of impressions? Perhaps design a business card with your portrait on it, or create (and rehearse) a compelling elevator pitch. Whatever you decide, create a strategy that makes you memorable.

References. As the meetings are short, you should come with a brochure, or an iPad. No one has the time to wait for your laptop to start up. If you want to show references, the file should be open and ready.

Brochures. Don't distribute large brochures. Potential clients have often travelled light and have no space for heavy brochures in their carry-on. You could even send it to them later. This gives you a nice opportunity for a follow-up contact.

CHAPTER 24
HOW TO CALCULATE A FEE

Learning how to generate effective fee proposals can make or break your practice. If you repeatedly generate low offers, you risk losing to competition, just as you risk losing if your offers are excessively high. To avoid this, let's start with the basics. Three main features compose a typical architecture fee. These are:
- staff costs
- overhead costs
- your profit.

In fee proposal terms, we are not selling designs in an architecture practice, but rather hours dedicated to a project, on a per-phase basis. Comprising the value of the hours are the above three components. For example, for a practice with three employees, the staff costs are the salaries paid, calculated as a per-hour figure. Add this number to the overhead costs (rent, coffee, etc.). This generates the internal hourly rate. How much you calculate for yourself per hour is up to you but, conservatively, it could be in line with the amount senior staff would earn.

Begin the fee proposal by estimating the number of hours needed for each staff member for each phase worked on the project. In the hourly rate for the staff, the overhead costs are already included. Now add project-specific costs, such as travel. This then comprises the full cost of the project for you. In addition to this, add a percentage for profit.

Base the profit on what you need, what the client is willing to pay and what the market allows. Defining all this can be quite challenging, but there are ways to confirm whether your fee is reasonable. To do this, check construction cost as well as historical information.

CONSTRUCTION COST
An architect's fee is always a percentage of the construction cost. With smaller projects, this percentage is normally slightly higher because work on a single family home compared to collective housing is less efficient. You can confirm with the RIBA or even google the percentages. Anything between 5 and 20% is reasonable, depending on the complexity of the work, the typology and the market. Be aware that this is solely about your part of the

work. There are books detailing construction costs, and on Building.co.uk, subscribers can find a lot of information. It might also be useful to check websites such as www.costmodelling.com.

HISTORICAL INFORMATION

The easiest point of reference is checking your fee proposal against fee proposals you have made in the past. If you don't have these references, ask colleague architects what they think of your offer. There used to be a mandatory fee system in the UK and other countries, including in France, where it's still valid to a certain degree. Some architects check their fee proposal against this (now ancient) system because it provides some indication of the number of hours per phase, which then provides an indication of the fee.

Summarising this very simplistically:
1. Make an estimate of the hours you need and calculate the cost of these hours.
2. Add all additional costs (travel, etc.).
3. Add a percentage for profit.

Sometimes architects have incredible luck, and have a contract that guarantees them a percentage of the construction cost of a project with escalating costs. An example of this is the Elbphilharmonie concert hall in Hamburg (Figure 24.1), with its mounting costs. Due to a lot of changes by the client and the necessary extra work, the fee for Herzog & de Meuron and their partners and subcontractors soared to over €90 million.[1] However, if the project is less expensive than expected, in some cases the fee declines. If you receive fees in a percentage, I would advise you to discuss a minimum. A fee based on hours, and not percentages, is less volatile. It's also important to make early agreements in the way additional work is remunerated, should the client make changes. To this end, articulate the changes the fee absorbs, and those that are additional.

See also Chapter 25, on contracts. The fee proposal and contract are closely connected.

Figure 24.1 *Elbphilharmonie Hamburg, Herzog & de Meuron, 2017. According to German magazine* Der Spiegel, *the architects of Elbphilharmonie Hamburg, and their partners and subcontractors, received a fee in excess of €90 million.*

PRACTICAL TIPS REGARDING CALCULATING A FEE

Additional work. Discuss at an early stage how the fee agreement defines additional work, and how it accommodates it. If additional work occurs, be sure to agree on the fee prior to starting this additional work.

Annual correction. Some project work will extend over a decade and in these cases, inflation reduces the fee. In the fee proposal, or contract, articulate in a clause that the fee rises according to inflation. Clients are often not happy about this clause.

Bad Cop. At times, architects have trouble negotiating a good fee because they fear ruining the relationship with the client. After all, you need to work with them for the next few years and you would hope that they are receptive of your exciting new proposals for their design. In this case, it can be smart to involve someone who will not work on the project in the contract and fee negotiation. For example, this could be your business partner, or even a lawyer. Some young architects hire an expert for a few hours. There are also business services that can manage this whole process for you. Although this service comes at a price, it pays for itself in the negotiation of higher fees for your work.

Check. If your fee proposal is accepted, act accordingly. Most practices that file for bankruptcy have cash flow problems. Stay abreast of the fee proposal, and send invoices in due time. Also, ensure that the hours worked are registered, and that you don't exceed estimated hours on given a phase. For any organisation that sells hours, this is the most important administrative practice to get right. To do this, closely monitor how many hours you spend to get the job done.

External hourly rate. The external hourly rate is the internal hourly rate plus the profit percentage. You can send this rate along with the fee proposal, to agree that you assign these hourly rates for additional work. Here the annual correction also applies.

Insurance. For complex projects, the insurance fee can be high, so don't forget to calculate this into the fee or the general office costs.

Internal hourly rate. This is the sum of all your costs divided over all productive project hours. This means that all costs are covered: from professional liability insurances to the coffee grounds, to all salaries, including the receptionist, any other non-productive hours and office rent. Sometimes a small risk and profit margin is included in the internal rate.

Invoice. Ensure that you receive payment for your invoices on time. The general advice is to put the pay-by date in a schedule so you don't neglect it. If the client pays late, put this three-step procedure in place: first, call your client to clarify why they have not paid their invoice; pair this with a formal reminder that the invoicing date has passed. In step two, you could send a letter that threatens to stop any work. In step three, you can stop the work and take legal action – which you want to avoid. Keep calling the client until the invoice is paid.

Invoicing scheme. Keep a schedule especially for invoices and make sure that it is always up-to-date, even if a project experiences a delay. Never forget to send an invoice in due time.

Last invoice. In many countries, the last invoice is the most difficult to receive. If you count on this, anticipate in the fee proposal that you won't receive the last invoice.

Negotiation. When sending the first fee proposal, it is wise to leave some room for negotiation, anticipating that the client will want to negotiate the fee down. Considering that this is likely, your first fee could be slightly inflated.

Phase. It's a great idea to get the beginning and end of a phase signed off by the client. This makes it official that you have completed the work according to the contract, and that a phase is contractually completed. This makes issuing the invoice a natural part of the contractual procedures.

Planning. As part of the fee proposal, planning is essential. In this planning, define the duration of each phase with milestones and key moments, such as approvals. Clearly define deliverables per phase. Invoice points should be part of this planning.

RIBA. Define your fee proposal according to the RIBA Plan of Work, and the standard RIBA agreements. For more information about making fee proposals, browse the RIBA website and perhaps sign up for a related workshop. It will be worth it.

Travel. If the project is a distance from your office, consider including travel costs in your fee, covering any distance requiring travel over one hour. You can include a certain number of trips in the fee proposal and then a lump sum payment for each additional trip. Don't forget that travel time is also time spent, so perhaps reflect this in the hourly charge for travel time by charging a lower rate for these hours (because they're generally not productive), but always charge for any time spent travelling over one hour.

This chapter was written with the generous help of Mariana Idiarte.

CHAPTER 25
CONTRACTS: MANAGING RISKS AND KEEPING PROMISES

Negotiating the contract for a project is without a doubt one of the most loathsome, but necessary, parts of the process. It's not unlike writing the prenuptial agreements before a marriage, when you are deeply in love and ready to commit, but forced to discuss a potential divorce. This is especially difficult for small practices, who often develop a close relationship with their clients. This makes talking about a contract uncomfortable and daunting.

Nevertheless, we need not debate how essential a contract is. We use them to establish the rules necessary to achieve a common goal (the project) and to arrange procedures should problems arise during the process. Finding a delicate balance between preparing for problems and not frightening clients in doing so is the trick. Use the contract to help create awareness of the fact that architectural projects are inevitably subject to (external) circumstances that can affect the ideal planning. With a thorough contract negotiation, you demonstrate how you'll manage these kinds of challenges if and when necessary.

Like a prenuptial agreement, investing some time and effort in negotiating a contract provides an opportunity for you and your client to get to know each other better. This helps you to understand the true, and potentially more personal, objectives you and your client wish to achieve in the project. It can also establish a strong precedent for future communication. There will be many times during a project that will require negotiation, whether for budget, aesthetic or functional choices. How the contract negotiation goes provides an indication of how you will manage challenging situations in future.

NEGOTIATING RIBA STANDARDS
In the UK, the RIBA provides a set of standard model contracts for architectural projects. In many countries, the local architects' organisation similarly provides standard contracts, which are usually well written, by architects for architects. Most of them are freely available to use, giving architects a solid foundation for use in practice. Alternatively, many architects use JCT's contracts.

In practice, many clients (particularly if they are professional or commercial clients) prefer to work with their own contract template and disregard the contract the architect proposes. In this case, follow the RIBA standards during the negotiation, and check the client's contract against the major topics outlined in the RIBA's standard contract model.

Independently of which contract format you agree to work with, a few of the basic subjects of an architect's contract that you should include are:
- definition of the scope of the work and the deliverables per phase
- distribution of roles and responsibilities, if there are other consultants (engineers, an executive or design architect, a contractor) involved in the project
- planning and phasing (including milestones per phase, meetings, presentations and the time the client needs to review and revert at decision-making moments)
- fee and payment conditions (to ensure cash flow and considering inflation, leading to a fee indexation, if the project will take long to complete or takes place in vulnerable economies)
- intellectual property rights: who owns these rights, how they can be used and under which conditions (this also applies to use of rights after completion of the project, to visit, photograph, reproduce and publish images of a project)
- indemnities and limitation of liability (and applicable insurance)
- suspension of the work and (early) cancellation: anticipating the reasons for suspension or possible cancellation, the consequences for the project and all parties, and the means by which you agree to manage risks
- additional work: definition of additional work (work that is not included in the agreed fee) and how the parties manage this
- applicable laws and processes for the resolution of disputes
- explicitly state confidentiality agreements, as well as possible consequences for a breach of contract.

During these negotiations, it is important to ask the client why they have included certain conditions. You might make assumptions but you need to find out what exactly they fear. Their insistence to address a particular issue can be an indication of their concerns, or of risks they suspect may arise. For example, by claiming the intellectual property rights, you might be anticipating that the client may wish to continue without you, while the client might actually fear that they will not be able to change the building in the future. If you discuss these explicit conditions openly and endeavour to understand the client's perspective, you might be able to address their fears in a win-win solution: add explicit terms that both maintain your rights, while addressing the client's concerns.

PRACTICAL TIPS REGARDING CONTRACTS

RIBA preferred. If you can, use the standard RIBA contract (or if abroad, other local standards). If the client suggests changes to the standard (RIBA) contract, ask which specific points are most important for them and focus on revising those only. The more you change a standard set of conditions, the more messy and difficult it is to interpret a contract. A transparent, clear contract is always the best starting point.

Wear the right hat at the right time. Some architects experience difficulty negotiating a contract and exclusively prefer to don their 'designer's hat'. They are worried about ruining the relationship with their client if they take on the 'negotiator' role. If this sounds like you, involve a third party to conduct contract negotiations with you, or on your behalf. A (business) partner in your firm, a contract manager or consultant, a lawyer or another team member that might have inherent negotiation skills can be effective to balance the roles and protect your position in the relationship with your client. If you are on your own, ensure that you separate the problem from the person. Also, ensure that the role you take in each instance (design meeting versus contract negotiation) is clear to the client as well. To this end, if you request a meeting to discuss the contract, make sure the client knows this, being careful to separate the conversation about contractual matters from project or design ones.

Take responsibility for the contract. The project leader in charge should know the contract more or less by heart. They must make sure the whole team is aware of the particularly critical matters in a contract, the consequences related to them and each of the team members' responsibilities, whether that is keeping to the agreed planning or complying with confidentiality conditions.

Begin work after you have a contractual agreement. Never start the work without signing the contract. Having a clear contract that both parties agree to is fundamental. In reality, you might be pushed to start on projects before you have signed a contract. If this is necessary, ensure there is an agreement of some kind. This might include a confirmation of an accepted services proposal, or a letter, signed by the client for acceptance, confirming the start of the work, and issuance of a down payment, to ensure cash flow, while the contract negotiation continues.

Consider bonuses or discounts as alternatives to penalties. Many clients include penalties for the architect in the contract. For some, postponement of payment is enough punishment. It is also true that penalties in a contract don't necessarily prevent delays or mitigate other risks. Nevertheless, try to understand the motivation for penalties. A delay might cost a project an investor, or the client could miss significant income in the longer term. To address this, propose alternatives to mitigate their risks: an incentive or bonus (instead of a penalty) if you deliver on time, or even better, earlier. You might also suggest a discount on your fee instalment if the client approves a phase with no delay. If there is no option but to accept penalties in the contract, ensure that these apply only if the delay is fully and completely your responsibility. Maintaining good records of documentation and communication with the client (as well as other consultants involved) is critical to protecting your position if others cause delay on your work or the project.

Check liabilities with your insurance policy. Many professional architectural contracts foresee a limitation of the architect's liability. Depending on the type and scale of project, this is likely connected to the amount (or a multiple) of the fee. In any case, liability in a contract should always be limited. Accepting unlimited (or unreasonable) indemnities or liability is a significant risk for your firm, potentially causing ruin. A project with high risks might benefit from a project-specific insurance policy, rather than the client placing all responsibility on the architect. You should not take responsibility for mistakes of other consultants you haven't contracted, or situations beyond your control. Saying this, in some countries it is impossible to avoid this. In these cases, the terms of liability in your insurance policy are critical.

Understand the difference between licences and transfer of IP rights. Intellectual property rights are often the topic of heated debate in negotiations. Clients feel they pay good money for your design, and that they have ownership rights. Even if most countries in the world agree that the creator is the owner of IP rights on a work, there is a common misunderstanding about what IP rights are, and how to leverage them. Ideally, you will be able to explain to your clients that you can retain all rights and, at the same time, provide them with a licence that (subject to certain conditions) allows them to use the design as widely and fully as they need to. If transfer of rights to the client is a deal-breaker, you should carefully consider applying clear conditions: not only full payment of your fees, but also limitations to the client continuing the project without you or building the project on additional sites. A contract clause deviating from the architect's right to own intellectual property should be written carefully, to protect the architect's interests in the project and avoid limitations to the use by the architect themselves.

Familiarise yourself with international rules and regulations.
If you work internationally, it's worth getting in touch with the local architectural association equivalent to the RIBA. They can help you with standard contracts and in understanding general rules of projects, as well as the architect's role in a specific context. Investing in the relationships with local architects in this regard is as important. They are a source of invaluable knowledge and information about working in their country. On the other hand, it is key to avoid generalisation. Every client and project is unique, independent of general assumptions we might make about their context.

Keep your promises. In contract negotiations, promise only as much as you can deliver. Then, ensure that you fulfil what you agree to. As simple and obvious as this may be, it is essential. Under-promising and over-delivering is as effective as over-promising and under-delivering is catastrophic. A breach of agreements on either side can result in lengthy legal battles and, in worst cases, bankruptcy. A thorough contract is realistic about what your practice can do for a client and a project. It is your means to assure clients that you are managing inherent risks and making the project they have in mind a reality.

This chapter was written with the generous help of Mariana Idiarte.

CHAPTER 26
IT'S NOT EASY BEING GREEN

The construction industry globally accounts for a significant amount of the world's CO2 emissions. This puts considerable responsibility on the shoulders of architects and planners to design in good conscience. In spite of this global urgency, in spite of the protests by young people and even in spite of the effects of climate change we personally experience, convincing clients to develop a building that contributes to the solution, rather than the problem, is no walk in the park. At best, we create buildings that cause less damage. Even then, this is not a holistic package, as it's either exclusively the construction or the maintenance or use that has certain sustainable elements.

Many architects articulate strong ambitions about their commitment to a CO2-neutral future;[1] some design buildings that generate more energy than they use, and there are those exceptional practices that consider the entire building to make it green. However, looking at the wider picture, I can only conclude that they are still niche architects: their turnover and production is miniscule compared to the larger volume that the rest of the construction industry accounts for. This critical mass still damages the planet. The West should be leading on this front, but land prices in central London, Paris, Melbourne, Amsterdam or New York are so great that architecture is often challenged financially, subject to cost and therefore less environmentally responsible.

There are exceptions to this, however. When the developers OVG decided to investigate sustainability for the new office building, The Edge, in Amsterdam's central business district, Zuidas, the architects, PLP from London, were able to max out the BREEAM scale[2] and achieve the first Outstanding in the Netherlands; it became a best practice project (Figure 26.1). The building is fantastic and innovative, and with the current speed of progress, even more is possible: for example, a building that fully adheres to circular-economy principles, as well as an energy-efficient building design that generates more energy than it consumes. Most buildings rarely go beyond legal requirements when it comes to sustainability. Clients often deal with so many other issues during design and construction that they are not eager to tackle the added complexities involved in achieving a truly sustainable project. Architects often lack

Figure 26.1 *The Edge, Amsterdam, PLP Architects, 2014. PLP Architects created the Netherlands' most sustainable office building, maxing out the current BREEAM scale.*

the necessary leverage to challenge this. This happens to all architects on all levels, except perhaps for those avant-garde niche architects, who explicitly produce sustainable architecture.

Trying to change this is challenging, yet important for us as a profession. Increasingly, there are opportunities in commercial developments, and room for argument, especially as far as business development is concerned.

Beginning with the basics: green labels such as BREEAM, and those used abroad such as LEED, HQE, Green Star and so on, support a strong marketing argument. They are not only sustainable but they also help the building to sell, which in turn enhances its reputation. For example, the entrance of One World Trade Center in New York bears an etching in its glass doors with the building's LEED label.

Certainly with less idealistic but profit-focused projects, the addition of sustainable elements can be challenging, but no less necessary. Speaking to the client in a language they understand, that is to say, connecting your green ambition and the ambition of the client, can be a powerful tactic to use. Create an argument and prove that the tenants or buyers will view sustainability as an attractive building feature, and that they will be willing to pay for it. You might also endeavour to find construction materials that are climate-friendly, circular or locally produced, at roughly the same price level as more traditional yet polluting materials. Perhaps you can specify a heating and cooling system with renewable energy production that reduces heating and cooling costs to zero. This is certainly a compelling feature for the building's intended end user or owner/occupant. In commercial projects, commercial arguments have the most impact with clients.

In public projects, which often remain in the ownership of a public institution, you might find a receptive ear to arguments focusing on maintenance and operational costs. This opens the door to green technology, as well as sustainable building materials. It may also respond to any targets that a local authority or other public client has set itself.

In terms of convincing a public body, 'green' arguments that support the city's particular mission can be integral to fast-tracking the project through planning, and garnering political support. For example, a building that filters polluted city air helps to support many current political agendas. A master plan for a district without parking, improving traffic flow through the city, can also be convincing. The inclusion of the 17 UN Sustainable Development Goals is a particularly compelling argument to present to a city council, as the goals are broad and tuned to enhance basic living standards for all citizens.

As with many issues discussed in this book, realising green goals for your projects, and making these part of the solution rather than the problem, depends on developing the right kind of communication with your client and strategically considering their interests.

PRACTICAL TIPS FOR GREEN ARCHITECTURE

Craft a green mission statement. If you want to make the world a better place, articulate this as one of your goals, and ensure that you, and your staff, act within this goal.

Begin with a clear PR strategy. Now that you have a clear green goal, communicate your thoughts and innovations related to this ambition so that clients with the same interest can find you. Be careful to practise what you preach. If you have a green mission statement, make sure you run your office in as green a way as possible.

Pursue relevant labels. If you have the time and budget, become a BREEAM or LEED Assessor, or have a staff member acquire accreditation. It will help you to design your buildings in line with these specifications and it is great PR.

Selling sustainability. Try to convince your clients with arguments that they understand. Commercial clients need commercial arguments and public clients want to hear how your green initiatives improve the public wellbeing.

Create remarkable projects. As is often the case in architecture, you need relevant references to acquire your next commission. Try in any way you can to design a sustainable project for your portfolio.

CHAPTER 27
THE PITCH

One of the easiest and most direct means of acquiring a new project is a casual discussion with a client. Many British architects I queried manage to do this over a pint. Alcoholic beverages appear to be the oil that keeps the British construction industry turning.

However, pitches are part of a more formal selection process. In this context, things are more serious because the client has probably already made a large investment in terms of time and money in developing the project, and the presentation you are about to give helps them to determine if you can make their dreams a reality. Here, you face yet another challenge: delivering the performance, presentation and communication acumen that will help you win the client over. If you perform well, a steady stream of work for five years awaits. If you mess it up... back home empty-handed.

Two contradictory claims about the elusive dynamics of the pitch might help you relax. At times, it happens magically and you win the commission within the first seconds of contact. This subconscious decision is comparable to a job interview. On the other extreme, you have the opportunity to impress with your content. If your design is exceptional, you can give a terrible presentation and yet still win the project.

So what can you do to convince decision-makers during a pitch? A fine example of such a battle is readily available online. This is Zaha Hadid, Richard Rogers, Norman Foster and Rem Koolhaas pitching for 425 Park Avenue, New York, in 2012. Watching their experience is incredibly educational because these four architects are the very elite of the discipline, and yet it seems that only one has truly mastered the technique of presentation.[1]

The presentations by Zaha Hadid, Rem Koolhaas and Lord Rogers seem to lack some understanding of basic presentation techniques. Both Rogers and Hadid shared the presentation with their partners but failed to explain why, they all sit in a darkened room to present and there is a lot of general talk about architecture that might not be relevant to the client. Koolhaas and Hadid even had small moments of negativity in their presentations, which could communicate to the client that the collaboration will not be easy.

Koolhaas, Rogers and Hadid studied the brief, and believed in the client's wish to create a landmark building. Both the selection of starchitects, and this brief, made them believe that this was the objective. However, the winner, Norman Foster, endeavoured to understand the essence of the project (equity), and he communicated this in an incredibly intelligent presentation.

Foster does not use a PowerPoint presentation, so he is in a room awash in light, whereas the other presenters are in darkness. He stands, works with panels and presents without a blazer. This is a dynamic and engaging set-up. He then explains that a landmark will come in due time and continues to explain the tower in economic terms, the floor plates and how it is a mix of 'design, market research and marketing'. He understands the details and gives a strong impression that he designed the building himself. This is certainly something that Hadid and Rogers fail to communicate. Oliver Wainwright, of *The Guardian,* writes the following about this contentious event: 'It is not hard to see why Foster so often triumphs. It is not only because he pedals a tried-and-tested brand, as a globally renowned safe pair of hands, but because he is one of the few principals of a practice this size with the ability to give the impression of having a personal grasp of every detail of the scheme.'[2]

Does the best design win? The most spectacular design certainly does not win, but Norman Foster wins the pitch battle. He appears more prepared than the others, not just in terms of content and in the hidden concept of the project, but also in terms of presentation technique. What is quite exceptional about this pitch battle is how poorly some appear to perform, and yet they are still the greatest architects with an enormous portfolio. Think about how much better you could do yourself, with adequate preparation.

It is very important to prepare well, to know who is in the room, and how the presentation will be conducted. The two-hander presentation format fails in this New York pitch, but it can be very effective if done well. If the senior partner radiates the image of an egalitarian office in which the principal supports his or her staff, then they can communicate this.

The pitch is not just the presentation of a building design; it answers key questions for the client as to whether or not they want to work with you for the next five years. They ask themselves whether they'd like a pint with you. I suppose this provides a good explanation as to why it's easier to pitch with a glass of something in your hand.

PRACTICAL TIPS FOR PITCHES

Make an effort to be convivial. If you get the chance, shake all hands (or the Covid-19 safe version) and frequently make eye contact with each person in the room during your presentation. Presenters have the tendency to look for interest in their audience, and then focus solely on the people who nod or look into your eyes. Try to avoid this, and address all who are present. It is often the people who seem less interested who you need to convince.

Personal presentation. As we witness in the pitch battle, you can present yourself in a stylish way, or in a no-nonsense way. Playing it safe, you might try to anticipate how the clients will dress and decide whether you will follow their example: fall in line, or stand out. There are advantages and disadvantages. In terms of personal hygiene, standards remain, so it is important to make that effort. Even if you had a sleepless night preparing beforehand, endeavour to look (and smell) your best.

Mind your manners. The pitch is a test as to whether or not you can work together for the next five years. You can lose simply by being nasty to your staff in front of the client.

Speak the client's language. Again, this is crucial. If the client is commercial, explain the project in commercial terms. If you want to discuss sculptural qualities with a commercial client, you could, for example, say that the design's sculptural qualities meet the council's requirements or that they might lead to higher rental income.

Discuss the client's explicit interests. If in the brief the client states certain interests, endeavour to mention them explicitly and respond. If the client wants a landmark, explain how your design will fulfil that.

Q&A. Although these are impromptu, it is also possible to prepare for the Q&A up to a point. Write potential questions beforehand and prepare responses. This is great training for the real Q&A.

Listen. You can lose by not leaving opportunity for the client to speak. If you refuse to listen because you only have a few minutes and you still want to make an important point, it can lead to the client thinking that if they chose you, you might never let them finish a sentence.

- **If in doubt, bluff.** If a question is unexpected, a little bluffing can help. For example, 'We thought about solution X, but we have not included it in this presentation.' Never overplay this. Be honest if there is no real answer, as you can always say that you want to do more research on this in the next phase, alongside your client.
- **Build trust.** You want to give the impression that you are capable of delivering the project, that you are experienced, skilled and that you will expertly manage the design challenge on behalf of the client in the best way possible.

CHAPTER 28
BROADENING YOUR PORTFOLIO

Many architects start their practice designing private residences or with even smaller commissions, such as extensions or loft conversions. Some never depart from this scope of work. According to the Architects' Council of Europe's 2018 report, 'There were 7,515 architectural practices in the UK: 4,407 of these were sole practitioners and a further 981 had just two staff.'[1] So according to these numbers, around 72% of all practices stick to small commissions and never grow beyond this.

In terms of architectural work, this is a sound strategy, as providing homes is the core business of the architect. This 72% sticks to the basics, and many of this number are happy and successful architects. However, if you consider this number from a business perspective the picture is less than rosy, meaning a majority of architecture practices are small and managing, but not necessarily thriving. In Germany, the Bund Deutscher Architekten (BDA, equivalent to the RIBA) has shared statistics indicating that sole practitioners earn an annual average of €45,000, while architects employed by larger offices earn on average €51,000.[2]

In this sense, it would be fair to conclude that expanding your portfolio in order to justify the employment of five staff members is, at least economically, a good strategy. However, this is far from easy. Nanne de Ru, of Powerhouse Company (see Case Study 8), is a great example of this. He broadened his portfolio to expand from private residences to larger projects, accomplishing this with a clear PR strategy of determination to grow the business. Carl Turner (see Case Study 7) transformed his architecture practice (renowned for a private residence featured on the Channel 4 programme 'Grand Designs') into a multidisciplinary, community-based practice that seeks out and realises its own projects. This is a truly inspiring twist. Not everybody succeeds in such a way. I have friends who began their practice with public projects but have since been stuck in commercial housing. In spite of their best efforts, they can't seem to escape.

If you have established a small practice devoted to private residences and loft conversions, it is far from easy to turn the tide and take on more or larger projects overnight. Willpower, entrepreneurial ambition and more than a little luck can make it possible. Certain external conditions are also integral to this. For instance, it's easier to succeed in a portfolio transformation when the economy is thriving. However, if the economy is thriving, you will be disrupting the office in busy times, so this is something you must be truly committed to if you choose to do it.

It takes a great deal of courage, a taste for risk and no small amount of willpower to turn around a portfolio. The temptation will be to accept a project of the 'wrong' typology, and invest your time and resources in this, because it's paying the bills. However, there are many examples of architects who have made the jump and have turned the page. You can also consider hiring staff to expand the business with the help of a new business partner to do the work that you already do, which might create time for you to go out hunting for different work.

PRACTICAL TIPS ON HOW TO BROADEN YOUR PORTFOLIO

Get out there. Do PR and BD directed towards potential new clients with your targeted project profile.

Participate in public tenders. Apply to public tenders, but ensure that they match your portfolio. To do this, you might have to start small. Moving from private residences to a small chapel, or bus shelter, can help to mobilise your transition.

Find collaborative partners. Collaborate with larger practices, but before you do, consider what kind of additional value you bring to the collaboration.

Investigate opportunities. Initiate your own projects, and build a development team to realise this, including a client, or initiate projects with residents of an area for which a city council might lend support.

Become an expert. Research the desired typology in a study and endeavour to become an expert, share your expertise at public events and lectures, and you may win some clients.

Go abroad. Sometimes in foreign countries, clients will accept your references even if these projects are of a different typology.

Go mixed use. Be vigilant if you see mixed-use projects. A private residence with a doctors' practice may open the doors to more utility buildings.

CHAPTER 29
PLANNING WORKFLOW

Some time ago, an architect couple with a small architecture practice invited me to lunch. Dining with them was like watching a Wimbledon tennis match: she spoke, he spoke, and by the end of it, I had whiplash. They had a great portfolio of work underway but this was only temporary, as in a few months there was nothing. She argued that they should take on work right at that point, and he argued that he had nightmares thinking of the amount of work they might have and not being able to deliver. I supported her argument for overbooking the practice, but he won the argument. Just a week or two later they were in trouble because, as is typical in architecture, a major project came to a halt and for a while they had no work for their staff. Luckily, they were able to reactivate a few old clients and take on new work.

Cash flow problems have prematurely caused the ruin of many bright architectural careers, so this makes planning essential. It happens to be one of the trickiest parts of running an architecture practice. For this reason, when I worked at OMA, I remember they had a special planning manager. This was a full-time role, whose responsibility was not only planning hours, but also managing the staff's special talents, and their ambitions. This was an almost impossible puzzle to solve.

Let's assume for now that an employee with a job is a happy employee. While in small practices this is not always the case, as the role does not always perfectly match the talents and desires of the employee, this is the perfect scenario to pick up new skills and enhance versatility. Let's discuss planning, with respect to generating a steady and manageable workflow.

A whole host of outside factors influence architecture projects, making planning completely unpredictable. As architecture practices are in the business of selling hours, every change changes the planning. In many architecture practices, this is in constant flux as projects, particularly in the early stages, experience frequent stop-and-go moments imposed by aspects architects have no control over.

If you work in this kind of dynamic environment, it is important to acknowledge this and overbook. If the worst comes to the worst, you will need to hire more staff and work harder. If you normally have a consistent flow of work, and something changes, it is important to have other means of weathering the stop of a project. Some architects excel at keeping clients actively waiting, so the moment a project stops, the clients waiting in line have good news. Nevertheless, I'd recommend that you have some financial buffer to survive a few months without work, and moreover, have in place a contract that mitigates this risk. Having a secondary business model running in parallel can be a great means of navigating gaps in your contracts.

Launching into rapid acquisition the moment that a project goes on hold because your planning is suddenly open can be an effective means of closing the gaps, but a certain degree of despair and desperation drives this, and hence it can be quite stressful. However, this despairing is great fuel to face your fear of cold calling, manage the trepidation you experience when reconnecting with former clients, reach out to potential collaborations or to network in order to meet potential clients.

If your planning and income rely on a single large project, I would try to monitor risks as much as possible and frequently assess and predict what could potentially stop the project, while also preparing what to do in the event that it does.

PRACTICAL ADVICE REGARDING PLANNING WORKFLOW

Anticyclical BD. It's a bit like a bank loan. If you have money, banks will loan you more. If you have projects, go out and get more. Overbook the practice if you are working in a highly dynamic typology or economy, or if the projects are risky and prone to delay by the council, etc. Plan more steadily if you are in a rather predictable business, while still preparing for the worst-case scenario and planning for how you will overcome it.

The contract. Define in your contract how to deal with delays caused by your client or third parties, to mitigate these risks. In spite of not working during this period, you can still receive payment for it.

Maintain a pool of flexible workers. If you overbook the practice and all goes well, great. You'll amass a profit, but you will soon find you need extra hands. Try to cultivate a pool of flexi workers who can help you in productive times, with the help of your network. Maybe even make a deal with a friendly architecture practice to be there for each other when necessary, to share staff.

Share good news. In times of need, you could call a client with news that you have a gap in your planning and that you can work on a project for them immediately.

Develop innovation in-house. If you have an annual budget for staff learning, the gap in the planning can be the right moment to use this time and encourage your staff to learn new software skills or develop other talents that will ultimately lead to a leaner workflow.

Feed and nurture your horse, especially if you've got only one. If you base your income on just one large project, treat it well, check its health and condition frequently, as well as the conditions of the road ahead. Consider the worst-case scenario, and prepare to replace this one big project if you must.

Establish a secondary business. Setting up a second line of income works for some architects. For example, some become Architects of Record for larger international offices, or model makers for other architects.

Do some urban planning. If you have the luxury to, bolster your urban planning scope. This can help to develop a steady flow of work, because many of these projects last a decade and generate a consistent, though low, income. Doing urban projects is one powerful strategy for filling the gaps.

Regularly update your planning. Consistently attend to your planning, and keep it updated. Do this every day if necessary, but at least once a week. This will help you predict your upcoming income and budget time and resources effectively.

CHAPTER 30
COLLABORATIONS

INTERNATIONAL COLLABORATIONS

If you worry about working abroad, finding the right partner is a great solution – in China alone, there are 2,000 highly experienced potential partners for you.

In 1992, MVRDV was a young and inexperienced start-up. From day one, they worked with a technical architect to execute all their buildings. This arrangement soon became standard, so the challenge remains that the level of detailing, and the quality of the built buildings, is to a great degree in the hands of the local architect. This means that selecting the right practice is essential because they will define and influence quality. If the choice is right, the collaboration can be incredibly valuable and seamless, creating a win-win situation in which foreign expertise and vision complements local customs and knowledge.

The local architect:
- facilitates the acquisition and lobbies key parties
- provides expertise about local building codes and customs
- completes construction drawings
- conducts site supervision
- bears legal responsibility.

There are challenges to overcome, and these can be serious. For example, the local architect and the client can develop a strong connection, so much so that they make decisions without you. Establish communication lines early in an agreement in order to determine how to collaborate and communicate within the combined team, and with the client. Also, if you consider the list of services that the local architect provides, it's 50% of the work and yet it's the practical work. It is important to defend your stake in the other half, and wield your ultimate decision power, avoiding a situation whereby you have two captains on the ship. Looking at it from a positive perspective, a collaboration with a local architect means that you can deliver a building according to the local building code. Isn't that something?

DOMESTIC COLLABORATIONS

As described in the Powerhouse Company case study in this book (see Case Study 8), strategic collaborations can be a means of growing your company and punching above your weight, by working on larger projects together than you would be able to run alone. Collaboration with an executive architect allows you to work on more projects at the same time, and to hire expertise you don't have within the studio.

Collaboration means that you work together, and not against each other. It's essential that you take time to develop a way of working that allows you to benefit from this situation, and not suffer from it. For example, work in one 3D model, and operate with the executive architect as principal, if you are both a single company. You should agree to be transparent, friendly and collegiate. The better you collaborate, the more successful the building will be, and the fewer chances there are for the client, or other consultants, to play you against each other.

Often the executive architect becomes a friend, so during the selection process it's not a bad idea to seek out alignment in terms of architectural thinking. Does the partner practice support your way of thinking? They don't need to make the same architecture as you but, later on, they might sit with a client and defend your design against budget cuts, so they should agree with your work. Including the partner early on in the process helps to create co-ownership and the entire process benefits from this.

Over the last two decades, I have built many teams for projects, and have noticed a clear trend towards collaborations, often interdisciplinary. Architects increasingly transform into being the coordinator of a large team of stakeholders and specialised consultants, so communication and collaboration become more important. There is a transition from engineering to a mediating and coordinating role. The downside is that architects split their fee with consultants and in doing this they lose traction. It is for this reason that the moment you become a larger firm you could – and perhaps should – reclaim some of the lost ground by adding internal specialists to your team who can handle, for example, engineering, sustainability and façades.

However, for a smaller firm, it can be great to outsource, and hire all the expertise you do not have, especially if the scope demands more esoteric disciplines, such as public participation specialists. Hardly anyone in architecture picked up this skill in university. You can focus on your design role if you hire external specialists for your team.

The key to a successful collaboration is making a clear agreement for the whole team and then treating the partnering practice as if they were part of your own.

PRACTICAL TIPS REGARDING COLLABORATIONS

Approach it like Tinder. If you like what you see, swipe right. When selecting a potential team member, think about the unique qualities they have and clearly define their role. If there is too much overlap between roles, and a gap in the overall expertise, refrain from collaboration. For example, two conceptual architects who then need a third to be executive architect is a recipe for disaster.

Establish a clear agreement. This need not always be a formal contract, but do endeavour to describe the collaboration between the two or more firms, as well as who is doing what, and who is going to decide what in which phase, etc.

Creating a Joint Venture. In the event that you need to establish a legal entity for the project, describe the decision-making process in the agreement, and clarify all risks that can emerge.

Drafting a contract. You may not work as an architect in some countries, so your role is design consultant. In this case, it becomes very important to describe the terms of collaboration, as well as the process for collaboration in the contract with the client. For example, articulate in this agreement that you can make decisions, have a right to veto all design-related issues and that it is you who determines solutions for changes, such as budget cuts.

CHAPTER 31
LEARNING FROM OTHERS

Aside from a few wonderful exceptions, there is little in architectural education that prepares architects to become successful entrepreneurs and run their businesses. This means that most architects who have succeeded business-wise are natural talents. These self-made men and women are often skilled autodidacts.

Each time MVRDV launched into a new phase, and needed business advice, the experts they consulted gave ready-made advice. This standard practical advice wasn't always applicable to architecture practices, as these tend to be quite particular. MVRDV grew frustrated with these £200-an-hour consultants, but thankfully we were able to turn to a large network of co-architects for advice, and we provided reciprocal assistance when requested. However, as their practices did not resemble MVRDV in size and scope, we lacked the precision of advice that a practice equivalent to ours might provide.

Faced with this frustration, and finding ourselves quite fond of the Scandinavian model of practice, we queried a number of large Scandinavian creative practices to determine whether they were interested in exchanging knowledge. To our great surprise, they all agreed. Despite the enormously competitive architectural industry, we experienced great generosity and collegiality when exchanging knowledge with other practices, many of whom are even direct competitors. We shared information about company processes as well as PR and BD structures.

The term 'competitors' is a difficult one. Are architectural practices competitors if they compete against each other once a year? When do they qualify as competitors? In the end, even BIG and Snøhetta agreed to some exchange, despite the fact that on a regular basis they are set against each other in competitions. The result of this exchange is reduced apprehension about the competition. In discussing details, we learned that in spite of these occasional competitive pairings, these architects ultimately have very different goals.

With this knowledge, and with the help of a tech company and artist studio, MVRDV compiled a book of best practice, which we printed as a hard copy, and lent to our principals as read-only. What we have learned is that we

Figure 31.1 *Events organised by the RIBA or other organisations in which peers exchange knowledge can be of incredible value to architects starting out, learning from those who have done it before them. In general, it helps the discipline to move ahead.*

cannot directly implement this knowledge in our practice. Instead, these other practices have great ideas that we have borrowed and transformed into policies or ambitions that suit our own company's culture. Perhaps they were being polite, but the other practices also agreed that the exchange was valuable to them as well. Provoking this kind of exchange and engaging in events designed to share professional knowledge can help move the entire discipline forward (Figure 31.1).

So, my strong advice is to find peers from time to time and exchange knowledge with an open spirit and learn from each other. If you can't organise exchanges directly, think about attending the RIBA events in your area.

PRACTICAL TIPS REGARDING LEARNING FROM OTHERS

Articulate your question. Defining exactly what you want to learn is the first step to finding the answer you're in search of.

Connect with the RIBA. Around the world, architectural organisations such as the RIBA, AIA, RCAI, BDA, BNA, UIA, etc. organise frequent events in which you can get practical advice from peers. The making of this book took root in a lecture during such an RIBA event in Bristol.

Select your medium of exchange. If you would prefer to exchange directly with peers in one-to-one conversations, network during the drinks after these events, and ask the odd question about something that challenges you. If that is too little time, perhaps make a list of practices that might have the answers for you. It does help if you have something to offer, so that you don't just go in search of assistance, but are open to a genuine exchange. Send an email, or pick up the phone and have a clear question and offer. Think about what's in it for them.

Pursue mentorship. If you are young and you have nothing more to offer than a fancy latte in a hipster café, why don't you connect with a mentor? This is a much more acceptable scenario for one-way knowledge exchange. Many professionals are flattered to be asked, and willing to share their experience. Because a mentoring trajectory is an intellectual exercise, it also helps the mentor. Mentoring challenges them to reflect, and this is usually the key to discerning new insights and business innovation.

CHAPTER 32
STYLES

After having discussed the need for collaboration and exchange in the previous chapters, this is also an ideal moment to discuss styles in architecture, as they have a strong relationship with business development and acquisition.

In terms of marketing, a recognisable style is a blessing. Look at the work of Andy Warhol. If you have a strong style you will sell your architecture much more easily than if you provide contextual architecture. Works by Zaha Hadid or Frank Gehry are easier to identify than works by architects with a less consistent portfolio. For clients, a recognisable style means clarity. It is a way to mitigate risk and, in terms of marketing recognisability, it is a strong argument. It is pure branding.

The downside is a certain predictability. What if your style runs out of fashion? As much as a set style is strongly recommended from a marketing point of view, many architects try to avoid it simply because it would bore or limit them. The priority is first the architecture, then to think about a way to sell it. If you admire a certain style, the best advice is to go for it and make the buildings as recognisable as possible. It's the golden rule of marketing. The interview with Phil Coffey in this book (see Case Study 4) shows how to find a balance between a strict style and a flexible approach that still connects the entire portfolio in an 'ethos'.

If you are a devoted postmodernist, you will attract different clients than a deconstructivist architect. This is because the work we produce appeals to different tastes. This is not limited to your taste and philosophy, but to your client's tastes and philosophies. These projects, whether peddling deconstructivism, blobism or postmodernism, will eventually be scrutinised in some way; if not by peers, perhaps by a competition jury or a city's aesthetics committee. In no other industry is work so ruthlessly debated by peers. Apple doesn't directly comment on the latest Huawei phone; however, architects often express their opinions on peers' work in interviews and other public forums. The debate about the 'right' kind of architecture can become dogmatic, almost religious, including manifests which declare parametric architecture as the only valid option, or in which traditionalists blame modernists and brutalists for unhappy cities.

Architecture is an applied art, and architects who design buildings for clients represent a small percentage of the total built environment. Consider the number of architects who work on practical projects such as infrastructure, industry and the vast no-man's-land of middle-class housing in developing nations. Consider architects who work for construction companies, property developers or within commercial brands, overseeing the construction of new shoe stores or petrol stations. Signature architects who embrace a certain style or methodology are a relatively small and exclusive group and the discussion in architectural media revolves around this niche product. Given this disproportion, dogmatic debates are potentially counterproductive to the discipline.

Architects and their critics would do well to respect the fact that architects serve their clients and projects within the scope and boundaries of that context. Why do we love to engage in debate about which style is the right one, while being permissive of brands such as Lidl or BP (and their competitors) who litter Europe and the world with their identically branded commercial buildings? Why don't we challenge the mediocre architecture produced en masse that despoils the architectural professional title? The architecture debate occurs at a very high level, and realising this might permit some tolerance. A traditional ornament on a building is at least an investment into something additional, and parametric architecture is a total engineering marvel that we can appreciate just for what it represents.

Architectural styles are transient and they leave traces on the history of a city, as a tree has rings. As much as people love to criticise brutalism, it is experiencing a considerable revival facilitated by no small amount of nostalgia. Which style is best? Your answer is an opinion.

My plea here is that, given the incredible scale of building produced without any real architectural expertise, we should consider the function of a building and test it on this premise, rather than on style. It does not mean that we should not be critical. Architectural critique is crucial to the discipline and should propel development, facilitate learning and prevent the worst excesses or mistakes. In a peer review, try to respect each other's differences and assume that the client and the architect have settled – for example – for a traditionalist design for good reason. Peer review should depart from this position, rather than an individual one.

This may be an esoteric perspective from someone who loves almost any style of architecture, but it is better for the business on a larger scale if your work on these committees focuses on content rather than opinions. We should value expertise rather than dismissing a style, and embrace diversity in architecture rather than demanding homogeneity. Peer reviews are public, or semi-public, and there is a great deal of leaked information and gossip about the process. It's easier to be rejected by an argument that is factual than by one based on opinion. Peers and potential clients take this advice to heart, and this has financial consequences. These critical arguments should be so well structured that the receiver feels they have been treated fairly.

More generally, when we criticise peers over stylistic differences, we fail to address the real problem, which is the fact that the vast, omnipresent majority of the building stock comes into existence without any attention to architectural thinking, yet we focus our critical discussions on a discrete minority, rendering our work more and more esoteric and intangible.

The American architect Marc Kushner gave an entertaining TED talk on the subject of the battle of innovators versus symbolists in architecture and how this has failed to be important.[1]

CHAPTER 33
ETHICS FOR ARCHITECTS

Architectural business development ethics play out at numerous scales, and the ethical choices a practice makes can have a lasting impact on its development and economic success.

In *The Edifice Complex*,[1] Deyan Sudjic poses a critical question concerning ethics in architecture. Sudjic's discussion chiefly concerns starchitects working on large projects, and supports the premise that the ambition for power compels these architects, because with power it is easier to realise sizable projects. Ethics are an everyday issue even in small to mid-size practices. In daily processes, there are critical decisions to make. The best among architects have faced them. Mies van der Rohe himself once had to decide whether or not he would work for Hitler.

Ethical practice begins with fundamental rules such as paying your interns and treating all employees fairly, as well as deciding how your workforce will represent the local demography, and to what extent you will implement equal-opportunity employment practices. You must also determine how you address overwork, and consider CO_2 compensation. Most importantly, you must consider the same ethical issues as those described in *The Edifice Complex*: decisions about who to work for and what kind of work to produce.

Ian Buruma once addressed a pressing ethical dilemma for architects working abroad, by claiming that it is fine to build a hospital, but that it is certainly not ethical – from a Western point of view – to engage in building prisons or central television buildings for an authoritarian state.[2] Most architects will never have to face an issue of this scale in their careers, but they will face their own moral dilemmas. For example, this might include deciding whether to make sustainable architecture, or deciding whether or not to build on the green belt. It might include deciding to design a project that exacerbates gentrification, urban sprawl and inequality. These are also deeply ethical decisions and may well influence your reputation in years to come.

Many Israeli architects I've met have made the decision to never work in the occupied territory. There is a clear line, and the choice is easy and deliberate. You're participating, or you're not. In Europe, the lines are not always so clear. For example, would you work for a high-street brand that has production facilities that employ child labour in developing countries? Would you work for a pension fund that invests in arms production? Would you work for a rich family that amassed its fortune in a post-socialist society? Is it okay to work for a company that pollutes the planet more than other companies do?

These are contentious points to discuss. At MVRDV, we made the decision to establish an office in China, but that does not mean that we condone all facets of this society. Instead we engage with this society from the inside, and do what we can to participate positively in its development. This might sound naïve, but we don't appreciate all qualities of Dutch society, nor do we condone our own colonial history. At the same time, we refuse to retreat into a purely ethical niche, because we believe that cities need excellent architecture. To this end, the world is not black and white, but different shades of grey. This position leads to discussions inside the practice, and these discussions provoke innovative ideas and design solutions.

For example, when a famous fast-food brand contacted us to design a new headquarters, we faced another dilemma. The site and the project itself were compelling, but the negative influence this company has on the planet was less so. We returned with a different proposal. Internally, we discussed what kind of building we would like to design for them, and thereafter suggested to

Figure 33.1 *Gazprom Neft, St Petersburg, Russia, MVRDV, second in the competition. Is it okay to work for a fossil fuel company? When faced with this dilemma in 2020, MVRDV decided to design the most sustainable building possible, using a timber construction. The thinking was, 'This building will exist anyway; let's try to make it green.'*

the client that we would design their headquarters if they would open the first ever vegan fast-food outlet on the ground floor.

Unfortunately, we never heard back from them. Creativity is a power architectural practices can exercise to endeavour to find a way to make the project ethically acceptable (Figure 33.1). Yet, can you afford to be so ethical? Once you make a decision, it can be unfair to criticise those who make a different choice. Either way, it's a difficult one.

An essential question to ask yourself is how your client has earned their money. Do we want to tell our kids that embezzled money, or money that is polluting the planet, or has been earned on the backs of children working in a shirt factory in a developing country, finances the breakfast they are eating? This is how you bring ethics home.

PRACTICAL TIPS REGARDING ETHICS FOR ARCHITECTS

Be authentic. Remain within your philosophy. Even if the project is highly attractive, don't step over your moral boundaries, unless you have a profoundly compelling reason. A feminist might not wish to engage in a building in Iran, but imagine you receive a commission to design a women's shelter in Tehran. Your decision might be different.

Talk about it. Discuss the ethical implications and issues involved in engaging in a commission within your office, and perhaps with friends who have a different political view than your own. This adds a new dimension to the dilemma.

Consider the implications. Discuss the possible consequences of ethical choices you make within your team. If you design a local Tory office, perhaps you'll no longer receive commissions from the Labour Party.

Follow the money. Endeavour to understand where your client's money comes from. If it's unclear, you can simply ask the client, or you could commission an agency to check credit ratings, and any other concerns you have about a particular client.

Be open. When it comes to ethics, it's important to consider the issue from two sides, and play devil's advocate. I found it useful to have different moral standards for myself at home and for myself at the practice. Realising that in private I am part of the confused and very dynamic electorate, I try to have an authentic and consistent ethical stance professionally, so that the ideas we propagate in the projects are supported by well-balanced ethical decisions that fit our mission and vision.

CHAPTER 34
SUING YOUR CLIENT

If you find yourself considering legal action, you have embarked on a nightmare situation. If you must, you must, as suing your client is sometimes the only means of saving your project and/or your practice. Architects rely on great relationships with clients in order to create architecture together, but a legal procedure potentially ends the harmonious relationship and can further jeopardise the project.

However, if we consider this from another angle, many clients impose fines for late delivery. Some clients sue their architects for all manner of design flaws in order to avoid paying their last bill. If buildings are faulty, clients sue architects to cover the cost of damages; most often it comes down to insurance companies to determine fault.

WHEN MIGHT YOU CONSIDER SUING YOUR CLIENT?
As an example, if your client withholds payment, you and your practice will suffer. If it is a question of survival, in pursuing legal action you have little to lose. In tender procedures, it can often be a welcome tactic. For example, if the calculation of the points is faulty, or if the winning project does not adhere to the brief, you may wish to challenge the decision. I once faced a situation in which we had unintentionally violated the rules of a tender by communicating with the client, who declared us winner of the competition, and then disqualified us. We went to court and won the case. The client, a public body, was happy with the legal procedure because they now had written evidence that they could continue with the project that had won the highest score in the procedure (ours), and they had a good argument to present to the second in line.

HOW DO YOU SUE YOUR CLIENT?
First, make every attempt to sort out the situation yourself, while carefully documenting every step. If this does not work, consult a lawyer. More often than not, the first discussion is free of charge, and thereafter the lawyer informs you of your chances, the potential cost of pursuit and further financial damages of the entire procedure. A lawyer will usually first draft a letter to your client before undertaking costly legal procedures.

You can help your lawyer by turning the legal procedure into an architecture project, because you probably know more about architecture than the lawyer does. When faced with an accusation of plagiarism, a well-known practice made a convincingly detailed analysis of the two projects, clearing the accused of every fraction of doubt, and even leading to a conviction of the plaintiff.

PRACTICAL TIPS REGARDING SUING YOUR CLIENT

Assess your chances. Within your firm, debate the chances of pursuing action, and only venture into a legal procedure if you have a great chance of actually winning.

Clarify costs. Try to obtain a clear concept of the cost of the legal pursuit, and determine if you can afford to undertake it. Only enter a legal procedure that you can afford to lose. Otherwise, bankruptcy looms.

Control your emotions. This is a difficult lesson to learn. Emotions should not cloud your judgement. Even if you are incredibly angry, try to discuss the issue in a neutral way, and play devil's advocate to view arguments from the vantage point of your opponent. This might lead to stronger arguments in your legal procedure. Decide beforehand if it is appropriate to show your emotions when in court. This platform can function as a theatre, so discuss this tactic with your lawyer. Sometimes a lawyer will argue that hiding your emotions might be better than getting angry in front of a judge.

Choose a lawyer wisely. Try to find a specialised lawyer and a lawyer who comes recommended by peers. There are, for example, lawyers who specialise in tenders, IP rights or construction.

Craft a clear PR story. Entering a legal procedure might make you look like a poor loser. In some cases, a clear PR strategy and storyline helps to address this. Imagine the effects on potential clients if your legal procedure hits the press. They might be inclined to think that you will sue them as well. To this end, your story must be so strong that any potential client would think, 'No wonder the architect sued. That was unacceptable.'

This chapter was written with the generous support of Mariana Idiarte.

CHAPTER 35
SPAM AND FRAUD

Perhaps this isn't necessary to mention, but it is important to be aware that the moment your company is registered in the Chamber of Commerce, an entire industry of fraudsters is ready to prey on you.

In the pre-digital era, we would receive fake invoices purportedly from the Yellow Pages or construction guides. The small print on the invoice indicated that by paying you confirmed a subscription, repeating the fraudulent payment many times over.

We encounter similar kinds of fraud in our private lives, such as spam, phishing emails and text messages, and we all must exercise caution. I know it's tempting, but don't believe that disgraced oligarch or the daughter of the president of Tajikistan who needs to use your bank account to secure millions of pounds.

A new kind of fraud targeting architects involves the invitation to design a library/museum/cruise terminal in one of the Emirates. The very formal-looking brief requests that you pay a few hundred pounds to obtain the tender documents. The clever thing is that these requirements are possible, so it is best to call the potential client or organiser, or perhaps your embassy in the location in question might be able to ascertain if the request is real. If you ever encounter this fraud, it may be wise to share this with the RIBA or the press, so they can warn others.

Also, a continual issue you'll face is callers inviting you to conferences with decision-makers in all kinds of exotic places. The call centre agents call you by your first name, make some flattering remarks about your importance, tell you which of your esteemed peers may also be participating and don't disclose any names of the magical decision-makers you will meet, while requesting a payment of £5,000. Best practice here is to ask for the conference's brochure and website and call peers who have agreed to participate to determine whether this conference is legitimate and worth your time and investment.

CHAPTER 36
CRISIS

Finally, crisis moments continually rear their heads in the course of a practice's career, with a real estate crisis emerging every so often. In the 27-year MVRDV career, the Covid-19 crisis is the fourth such moment we have faced, although it is unprecedented by comparison with the others.

Reading newspapers such as *The Economist*, the *Financial Times* or their local equivalents ensures that we have a clear picture of the business climate and can predict when a new crisis might materialise. Covid-19 came without much warning, and with it, profoundly unpredictable future scenarios, within which the UK economy might plummet by an unprecedented amount, and many jobs are at risk globally. We may never get back to normal, say some commentators. As I write these lines, we don't know what the future holds, but we must deal with uncertainties, yet again.

The first crisis MVRDV's founders faced in the Netherlands was in the early 1990s. The three founders were then employees of larger firms who had reduced their hours to part-time contracts. They used this time to win the Europan competition, and thereafter established the company. The burst of the internet bubble in the late 1990s hit the practice. The office laid off staff and thereafter endeavoured to organise finances to prevent similar strife in future. The global financial crisis in 2008 contributed to a complete downturn at home – the Dutch market collapsed. So enhancing our international profile and expanding the portfolio to include new typologies, as well as urban planning, became increasingly important. The crisis also fuelled professionalisation, including BIM, BREEAM, LEED and all sorts of growth and improvement of service offer. Each crisis yields a new kind of growth and development, but in turn, each threatens survival.

Hit by the prospect of yet another crisis with the Covid-19 pandemic, we hypothesised different scenarios that could influence the company, by making financial overviews a weekly discipline and writing emergency plans for operations, public relations and business development. For example, faced with the cancellation of MIPIM and other real estate fairs, we had to pursue alternative means of meeting potential clients.

Figure 36.1 *During the Covid-19 pandemic, BIG architects, New York, used their 30 3D printers to produce PPE for hospitals, showing great social responsibility in a time of crisis.*

Taking a crisis seriously and devising decisive strategies is probably the best – and yet generic – advice I can provide when facing a crisis. It's basically a puzzle. If your domestic market evaporates, as it did for us in 2008, how can you address this? If demand for your main building typology falls, or your largest project falls through, how do you manage?

The moment the Dutch Government began to discuss the implications of companies needing to restrict interaction to 1.5m during the Covid-19 pandemic, many architects advertised new services to quick-fix existing offices, transforming them according to social-distancing regulations. Others began to produce PPE equipment for hospitals using their in-house 3D printers, a wonderful means of supporting undersupplied hospitals, and a powerful PR strategy that features the soft side of these practices and their commitment to social responsibilities (Figure 36.1).

For young architects starting out, there are inspiring examples for not only surviving but also flourishing during crises. The Powerhouse Company case study (see Case Study 8) is a striking one, but there are other stories of architects who have become place-makers or even legal squatters, and in the wake of a crisis, landlords. Seeking out opportunities and endeavouring to survive a very profound crisis is not easy, but it is possible. However, in addition to talent and determination, you need a bit of luck, as it is impossible to control all factors. Failure is part of being an entrepreneur, and there is no reason for shame, as long as you do all that is within your power to survive.

Good luck and stay safe!

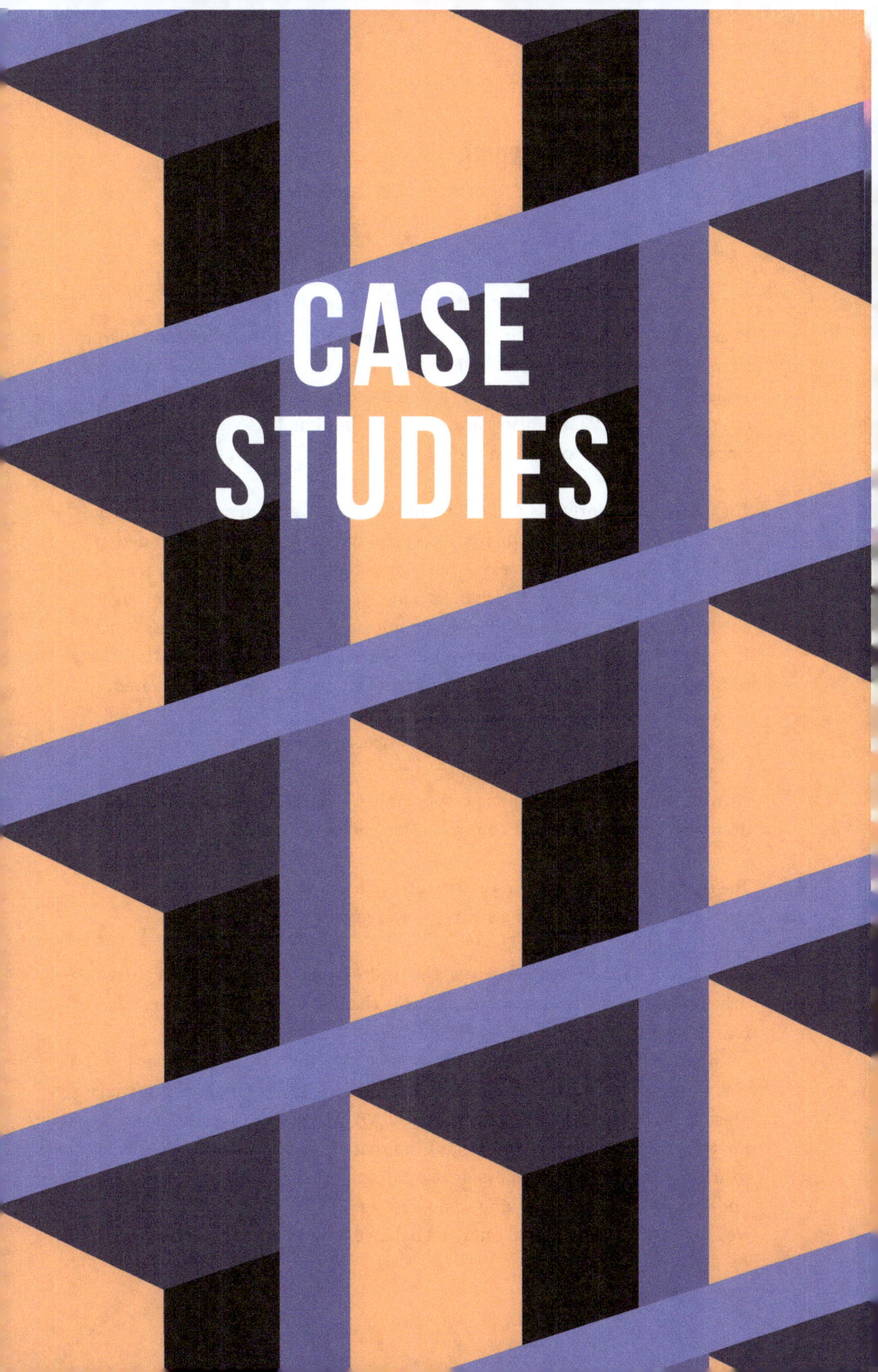

CASE STUDY 1
SHEDKM – HAZEL ROUNDING

'Don't be afraid to talk about business.'

As part of doing good architecture, it's also important to have a good financial balance.

Upon entering the offices of shedkm in Liverpool, visitors' eyes are drawn to a large floor-to-ceiling portrait of Le Corbusier surrounded by bright yellow walls. shedkm have always believed that modernism is the perfect design approach for the 21st century and they use the signature yellow on their website, in their office and on the odd building.

The practice currently has 45 staff members in total and, in addition to their head office in Liverpool, a highly successful branch in London. Founded in the 1990s, in their first 10 years of existence the firm embarked on a fruitful strategic collaboration with Urban Splash, which generated many projects for shedkm until the communal portfolio comprised 90% of the practice's work. However, their robust portfolio took a hit when the UK suffered from the effects of the 2008 financial crisis. Almost overnight, the portfolio disappeared.

'In some ways, we are a 22-year-old practice, and in some ways – thanks to the crisis – we are only 10 years old,' explains Hazel Rounding, one of the six directors of shedkm, who is responsible for the business side. 'It was a dramatic situation: we had 24 mouths to feed, and no work.'

The practice then decided to restructure, equalising the six directors. Thereafter, they developed a strategy to diversify the portfolio.

As is the case with many practices, the desire to create great architecture drives shedkm's work. Rounding explains that Dave King, one of the founders, is 80 years old and still visits the office to mentor young architects. In this context it can be challenging to discuss the business side of architecture, yet Rounding shows me a very sophisticated internal presentation (yes, with the signature yellow), which explains just that. Rounding made the presentation for her team to explain what she is trying to achieve in terms of business development. 'I think that people need to understand what we are trying to do, and as part of doing good architecture, we also have to have a good financial balance,' she says.

Figure 37.1.1 *Ruskin Square Project, East Croydon, shedkm, 2016.*

Maintaining a sizable office that is able to take on larger commissions is part of any successful business strategy, and opening an office in London to be closer to the larger clients was a smart move. This has created new opportunities for the practice.

Rounding explains how architects who excel in architecture are often less talented in business and lose to architects who are good in business but produce poor architecture. This is not what shedkm wants to achieve, Rounding argues. 'As a group of people, we have never been interested just in profit, but we learned to be also a good company, next to being good architects.'

The tension between the purity of architecture and business development is noticeable. On the one hand, Rounding is clearly enthusiastic about the business side of architecture, she has a clear business strategy, a spotless presentation and she advises developing firms, 'Don't be afraid to talk about business.' Yet, at the same time, she is a practising architect with no aspirations to carry the title managing director. During the conversation, she continually returns to the work and the essential philosophies of the practice, clearly indicating that a discussion exclusively about business is insufficient. Without a doubt, architecture is shedkm's main priority; operating as a business is incredibly important, but it simply supports the practice of creating architecture.

The practice acquires new work through meetings, presentations, collaborations and sharing references, as the architects retain contact with potential clients and try to meet as many as possible at places such as the MIPIM. Sometimes, Rounding explains, a project is the result of five to ten years of networking.

Caro Communication, an architecturally savvy PR agency, contributes to the practice's PR. shedkm has a wonderful online presence, and their upbeat posts add to their reputation as a friendly, active and humane office. In 2020, a 'before and after' series illustrated their renovation projects both in the present and before the renovation (in historic black-and-white photography), creating a beautiful impression of timelessness which was well received on social media. When asked whether their social media presence delivers new projects, Rounding states that it allows the firm to remain present in the consciousness of clients and stakeholders, which is undoubtedly a sound argument for an active social media presence.

CASE STUDY 2
MGMASTUDIO – MATHEW GILES AND MATTHEW ASHTON

'We decided to become patrons of Liverpool Philharmonic.'

Relationships and branding that builds community.
The MgMaStudio office is located in Oriel Chambers in Liverpool, the first building in the world to feature a metal-framed glass curtain wall, whose construction in 1864 marked the arrival of the skyscraper. Sober, dark tones define the office space's tasteful interior impression. The two principals, Mathew Giles and Matthew Ashton, are not just distinguishable in their single or double 't', but also by their opposing characters and descent, as a northerner and a southerner, respectively, who run a successful studio in Liverpool.

When the two architects founded the company in 2011, they deliberately selected Liverpool. The city had cheap rental spaces on offer, an absence of a heavy corporate culture and – being a World Heritage Site – an abundance of historical structures in dire need of maintenance and transformation.

Establishing the practice was in part a reaction to their first job experiences at a practice that had little interest in business development. Hence, they founded MgMaStudio with an orientation supporting the idea that an architecture practice is also a business. The two partners took an EU-funded, one-week crash course in becoming entrepreneurs at John Moores University, wrote a business plan and when the week was out, established their company. 'We signed the lease, bought a car, computers and printers and we wanted to get to work,' explains Giles.

'Unlike many other practices, we made the decision not to start from a bedroom,' Giles continues. 'You can't bring your clients to a bedroom. It might be fun for some, but it's not professional, and we wanted to be a serious business.'

In the beginning, acquisition was their main priority. Their success was mainly based on the fact that Liverpool is a very social city, with a strong oral culture, and meeting people face to face is incredibly important. To this end, they appeared at any event they could think of.

'We endured three years of canapés, Peronis and croissants, and these three years must have shortened our lives by five at least,' Ashton jokes. Giles adds

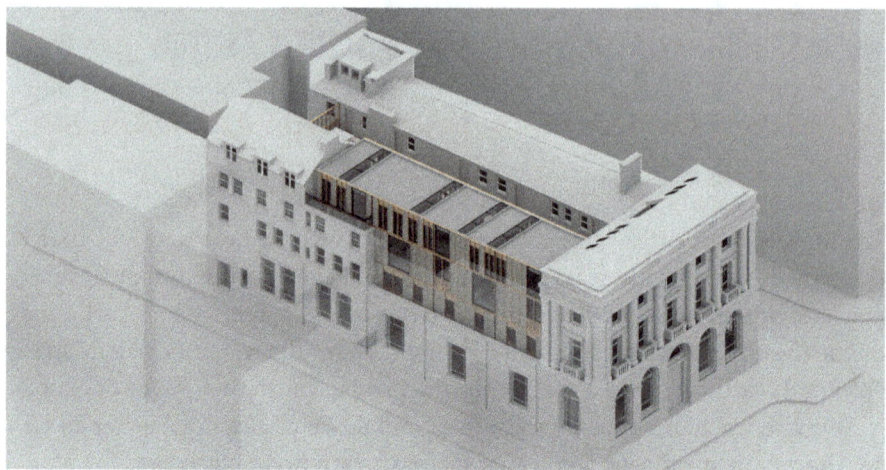

Figure 37.2.1 *Water Street Liverpool, isometric view, MgMaStudio.*

that in the first years they lived on 'beans and toast with cheese on Friday as a real treat'.

At this point, acquisition drove the studio, with Giles and Ashton having underestimated just how bad the economy was. At the onset of their practice, the need for work was the only strategy in terms of portfolio building. The challenge was enormous. 'If liquidity dries up, as a small office, you are at the bottom of the food chain,' says Giles.

What helped to distinguish them was picking up some conservation projects, first by helping with small jobs, and then slowly transforming them into a built portfolio that led to increasingly larger and more prestigious work. Their first project of this order, a listed Georgian townhouse conversion, was helpful as it provided their first built reference. Doing acquisitions without built references was very difficult, and in terms of marketing, the architects did not take the easy route. Giles explains that they simply 'refused to speak about our previous life as employees because we wanted to be independent. From a marketing point of view, this seems suicidal. For example, I never told people that I did complex planning applications on my own.'

Acknowledging the social nature of Liverpool, and to grow their network, they set out not only to network at social events, but also to organise them in their office. Their 'Prosecco Fridays' were a great success. Without a marketing budget, they became inventive: lights off in the office, music on – the streetlights and street life animated the space. Each time, they bought six bottles of Prosecco, some tapas and invited interesting multidisciplinary people with the instruction to bring a bottle with them, under £10.

Giles explains, 'As we got around making these relationships, we realised that they don't know what architects do. We offered them a look behind the curtain of what we do in our office. We chose this office because of the ambition of the space. It's a great space to socialise and these Friday evenings often were long, five to midnight.'

The multidisciplinary guest list was also useful for the guests, says Ashton. 'Often the architect is the connector between other disciplines; we could take this function, advise people to connect and built up relationships. It's amazing how many cross-sector friendships developed during these Friday nights.'

The creation of a gang of people in various disciplines was the key to future projects. MgMaStudio discovered that branding, for them, was to build a community.

From the niche of conservation, other projects emerged and, as before, small projects often led to a relationship with a client, which ultimately led to larger commissions. Still, 80% of the portfolio is made of refurbishment work, the most common on offer in World Heritage Sites like Liverpool and Manchester, cities with the lowest rate of dwelling replacement in Europe and hence a very tight market for new architecture.

In order to connect with the clients, they developed a great new marketing approach, again fully in line with the social character of their location. Giles explains, 'We asked ourselves, how can we connect with the decision-makers who are older than us? We needed to propel ourselves into the generation of our parents without having their network here. Mum and Dad aren't here, so how to do it? We decided to become patrons of Liverpool Philharmonic and started to meet them in their surroundings.'

Ashton says that it was not strategically planned, but it became a great strategy. He adds, 'All these little things we did, and do, add up to where we are now, working with the National Trust and doing relatively prestigious projects in a tight market.'

Being a small firm, Giles and Ashton offer their own time, as directors, to clients and they see this as a great advantage over larger companies, which have to send employees to the table. Another advantage is the fact that the two directors are opposing characters, which widens the spectrum of potential marketing. Ashton is the more introverted, technical type and Giles, who is extraverted, can offer clients a story and a journey. Both characters attract different clients.

Local presence comes with a certain responsibility, according to Ashton, who engages in a local advisory board. In addition, both partners teach at the University of Liverpool. 'You need to offer your expertise and you need to offer active interest in the places you live; this investment will also help you to build up your business,' says Ashton.

With the practice nearing a decade 'old', it was time to invite a branding agency to redefine and reposition them. The agency got under their skin and asked many difficult questions, with the aim of finding the soul of the practice. Having a history of nearly 10 years and the responsibility of supporting five staff members meant that the freedom to change direction was limited. However, the need to change arose from the belief that if the learning curve stops, a practice might get lazy. Therefore, further development has become their goal.

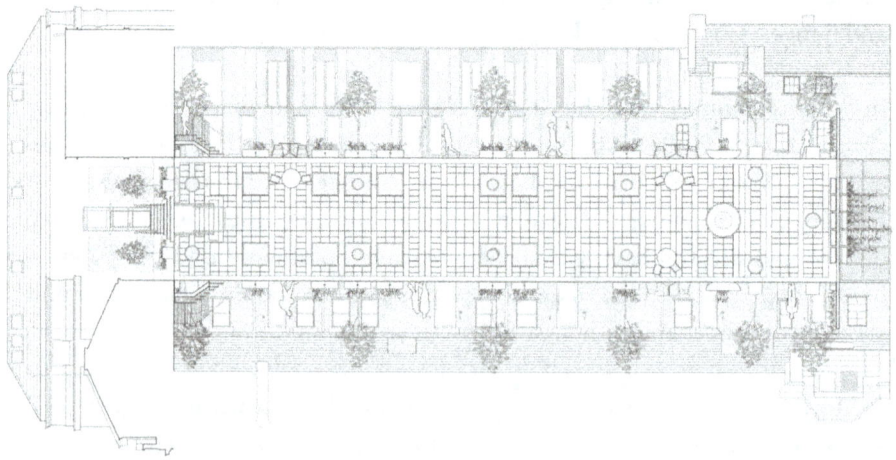

Figure 37.2.2 *Water Street Liverpool, courtyard, MgMaStudio.*

CASE STUDY 3
STUDIO MUTT – JAMES CRAWFORD

'We got a lot of interest; it then snowballed into other jobs.'

Instagram's shooting stars

Down the corridor from face-to-face marketing champions MgMaStudio at Oriel Chambers, in Liverpool, is Studio MUTT. A young practice established in 2017, they have an entirely different approach to procuring work, having already been commissioned by an array of important clients such as the Sir John Soane's Museum, the British Council and the V&A.

Their suite is colourful and bright, and furnished with Studio Job objects. It communicates good humour and makes a strong connection between the portfolio, the website and the interior of the practice: all of which are joyful and happy. Here, they embrace the power of social media for marketing purposes. Thanks to a portfolio of photogenic projects, and artistic and sometimes provocative collages, Instagram significantly enhanced their reputation, leading to instant success. This was not by happenstance. Instead, the three founders of Studio MUTT, Graham Burn, James Crawford and Alexander Turner, made an important strategic investment.

Having been friends since university, the trio first acquired work experience at larger practices, with the clear goal to establish their own studio. While in full-time employment, the three friends spent evenings and weekends working on competitions. To their great frustration, they would be shortlisted, but when it came to convincing the client that they had enough experience, they could not provide sufficient evidence with built work. This led to disappointment – despite having been able to show earlier work experience in different architecture offices.

When they had an opportunity to design and build a small pavilion in the Lake District for the staggeringly low budget of £12,000, they grabbed at it, and became incredibly hands-on, designing, building and installing the Ordnance Pavilion all by themselves. *Dezeen* and the *Architects' Journal* spotted a post on Instagram featuring the project, and they both contacted Studio MUTT to request a publication. This gave the company a head start.

Studio MUTT's directors are well aware of the power of PR as it led from one opportunity to the next. 'We got a lot of interest; it then snowballed into other jobs. I suppose from being published on Dezeen you get a lot of interest, which is very nice,' says Crawford.

Appearing in the *Architects' Journal* was also helpful, and the pavilion was nominated for an award, which increased its visibility even more. 'We still get enquiries two years on,' Crawford says.

Crawford believes that in terms of the time the three architects spent on the pavilion, the project was a significant but worthwhile investment. He states, 'Small projects have the advantage of being fast and immediate. I suppose the difficulty after such a big start is how to move on from this to more serious commissions.'

They chose the name Studio MUTT, taking the name of a beloved mixed-breed dog due to their wide-ranging interests in art, exhibitions, fashion, architecture and interiors. Currently the practice is working on a sizable hotel project opposite the Three Graces in Liverpool, in a historically very sensitive location at the entrance of James Street, facing Albion House. Here they faced the stark reality of working in a professional context, having had their very joyful initial scheme tempered by the influence of the heritage authority. Nonetheless, the young architects have, only a few years into their practice, an impressive and quite seriously sized project. This is a rather unusual feat in the days of stringent European Tenders and risk-averse clients who blindly trust repeated experience.

They acquired the James Street hotel project through existing business relationships. Besides this direct approach, Studio MUTT also use pitches and competitions to acquire new work. However, the power of social media continues to work for them, and they ensure this by employing graphics with a distinctly joyful, artistic style. 'We like montages for their aesthetic quality and because they are quick,' explains Crawford, adding, 'Models are the best tool to convince people. It surprises me how little people sometimes understand if we don't work with models. We make a montage and then we realise that they don't understand it. I suppose people are not trained in looking at visuals. In this way, the model is supportive.'

Where other studios oscillate between artistic presentation for institutional clients and more commercial renders for the public, Studio MUTT prefer to work with models in order to ensure understanding. They developed a large model for a project for the V&A in London and this happened to be a great means of convincing the client. They acquired other projects, such as a park in Camden, through their social media activities, and once got a commission on a shopping trip. In terms of marketing, for now MUTT are in the early phase of their career, and use all manner of available channels to get in touch with and meet new clients, both proactively and passively, as they have also been successful through publications.

The three directors work on all project phases. 'Unlike in football, we like to play in all positions,' Crawford explains. Yet there are some specialisations emerging, loosely based on their talents. Burn, for example, is the writer of the trio.

Figure 37.3.1 *Studio MUTT, Ordnance Pavilion on social media.*

As much as they can attribute their initial success to social media, the entire operation of the practice relies on modern technology. Located in both Liverpool and London, the three architects work together closely on each project, despite their physical distance. Without a cloud-based server, and long sessions on FaceTime, it would be impossible to work in this way.

Being a young practice, the standards the RIBA provides concerning fee structure and contracts, for example, help them to maintain robust business processes, first established in an initial business plan. They are cognisant of risk aversion, and reducing financial dependence on a single project. Being connected and open-minded means that the architects have also realised their first temporary project in Mexico and created a plan for a building in New York. Working abroad seems the natural next step, though it is not an explicit ambition. If the opportunity presents itself, they will evaluate it with an open mind.

Crawford and his two partners are holistic architects of the present, in the sense that they have fully embraced the amazing array of potential and responsibilities architects must face in practice, and they realise that these are still early days. According to Crawford, 'It's a work in progress to develop a practice culture and a way of working.'

CASE STUDY 4
COFFEY ARCHITECTS – PHIL COFFEY

'I want to be structurally ahead, that is the essence of investment.'

Punching above your weight.

Of all the architects I have interviewed while writing this book, Phil Coffey is the only one who was accompanied by his head of PR (Margaret Ravenscroft). This reveals the duality of Coffey's force; besides being an architect, he is interested in the ephemeral side of the discipline – people, culture and light – while also being a keen business leader.

Punching above his weight is a way of life for Coffey, who founded the practice on his own, after having done enough 'resi stuff' on the side, in addition to his employment, to become financially stable for half a year. 'Founding the practice meant a leap from projects with a budget in the millions to doing projects with a budget in the thousands,' he explains.

After working on small projects for the first five years, he began to win awards. Receiving the '40 Under 40' award was a career changer for him, as it has led to more residential and developer-led projects. When he won a competition for the St. Patrick's School music room and library, in north London, in 2011, he ascended the ranks with the RIBA Stephen Lawrence Prize and a range of awards for best small buildings. This was a moment to step forward with acquisitions, go to MIPIM, meet people and be seen. These activities in turn have led to more projects.

This progress adheres to a clear strategy. At every stage of the practice's development, Coffey locks himself in a room to consider where the journey should lead, and determine the next stage of the development.

Staffing has become an essential means of investing in his practice. Hiring a Chinese architect led to his first foreign acquisition, a 40,000m^2 project in Qingdao. 'It was helpful doing such a large project in a foreign land. It showed that we understood strategy and that we could do larger scales, also at home,' says Coffey.

From this moment on, the practice won competitions for larger projects. Another investment in staffing came as a result of reactions from his clients.

Figure 37.4.1 *Apartment Block by Coffey Architects. London, 2019.*

Coffey describes this learning experience as follows: 'You have me and my baby-face, and then you start to get into bigger meetings with bigger clients and they look at me and my ability to sell stuff. They also look to my right, and left, thinking who do they have to talk to every day if they do the project with me.'

So Coffey decided to hire two experienced architects, older than him: 'Not that we could afford it necessarily,' says Coffey, 'but this is what investment is all about. You invest money into your own future. I want to be structurally ahead, that is the essence of investment.'

Having two experienced project directors and a head of PR makes the 24-person practice a serious player, despite its relatively medium scale. 'With this structure, we are set for growth. We can grow now up to 40 to 50 people within the current set-up. I also like to think about what's holding back the practice, and how to solve this,' says Coffey.

Coffey recognised at a certain moment that having a practice established around its founder was holding him back. For a while, he stopped drawing because he noticed that his team would then simply execute his drawing, whereas he wanted to encourage them to think for themselves and design something smart. He became an editor for his practice, as he believes there are various ways to design: with the hand, with the brain and with the mouth. After the practice had established a common sense of design ethos, he began to draw again. 'Recently I have been getting back to drawings,' says Coffey. 'When you get to a certain scale and client, they want you in the room and I noticed that they like the hand drawing. Sketches with hand drawings work very well; it creates a fast and flexible design process.'

For a long time, acquisition was Coffey's challenge. 'To get new work, I go out losing my liver,' says Coffey. 'I spent a lot of time out and about.' This works well for private clients, yet the practice is following a successful strategy of diverting into more sectors, such as commercial housing, libraries, cultural buildings and, more recently, even urban design. 'I think it's important to keep the spread because it's interesting,' says Coffey. Yet in acquisition, it's a challenge. Coffey says, 'Three or four years ago we'd receive a phone call and we got the job; now it's all about mini competitions. Luckily, we are good in winning them.'

Part of being good in acquisition is also developing a talent explaining references effectively. Instead of simply using standardised explanations, the practice became expert in explaining the principles of their reference, and what these principles mean for the project they are in the process of trying to acquire. This is an intelligent means of addressing tenders that demand identical references.

Explanation is integral in acquisition, to ensure that the clients understand relevant features of a practice's projects. 'It's not in my skillset, so I thought, why not leave it to a professional,' says Coffey. For this reason, the practice brought Margaret Ravenscroft on board. She explains that it's a waste of time for architects to do their communications activities, as they have better things to do. Her network and experience make the task faster and easier.

When asked whether the practice works for free, Coffey corrects me and says, 'I would not call it free work. It's an investment in winning the project.' To this end, they evaluate their chances carefully, and point out that for small projects, an investment can even be counterproductive. 'The clients of smaller projects like your work better if they pay for it,' says Coffey. However, larger commissions benefit from testing the waters and building trust with a sketch.

Unlike many other architects, Coffey fully embraces PR and marketing as tools and he believes in the concept of branding. 'Architecture is a business and, as such, you need to do PR and market your business,' continues Coffey. 'It's easier to market work if it's consistent, because clients know what they get.'

However, this does not lead to a strict style. He refers to the practice's work as having a common ethos. He explains, 'The practice was about me for a long time. It was about my personal motivations regarding the planet, light and photography. In order to prevent potential limitations, I have had to let it go personally and replace it with the ethos. Let me explain, I am doing a PhD in light and I involve the praxis in it, so it becomes a communal project, which will influence the practice. It will be connected by an intellectual idea, by a way of thinking which I see as a brand, and which is highly authentic in reflecting our beliefs.'

The ethos then becomes a way of thinking applied by all staff in the practice, leading to a consistent output. This is visible on the website, as the projects all share a common vision and perhaps a certain contented modernism. Very important to Coffey, the photography is consistent. 'I always work with the same photographer, Tim Soar,' he says. 'This is incredibly important. Few people visit our buildings, which makes the photography essential. In Tim's work is a continuity of lines and geometry that he picks up and it's light-led. Architecture is about things you can't draw, it is about lights, shadows and thoughts. Think about that.'

Figure 37.4.2 *Hidden House by Coffey Architects, London, 2017.*

CASE STUDY 5
DMA – DAVID MILLER

'The challenge for us is to distinguish ourselves in an oversupplied market.'

A different approach to marketing.

When he first set up practice in central London in 2001, David Miller soon came to realise that he was in one of the most competitive architecture markets in the world. 'Around our office, we once determined that there are 30 architecture practices that all share the same postcode. Within a few streets are likely a thousand qualified architects, all good in design and in selling it.' Having previously worked in the offices of Norman Foster, Santiago Calatrava and Future Systems, he was well aware of the need for architecture practices to distinguish themselves. 'We thought long and hard about our unique quality. The challenge for us is to distinguish ourselves in an oversupplied market.'

DMA set about defining their particular specialisms and talents, and the things they do better and differently to others, and started to build and imagine the practice around these core qualities.

One of these is their relationship with technology. 'We were early adapters. Having worked on complex technological projects before, we were technical and computer savvy, and technologically literate,' says Miller. This meant that, even in the very early days, they were given projects that were difficult to deliver – for example, one of the practice's first projects was completing a concept design by Ushida Findlay, involving the insertion of a curved pool house between two Grade II listed farm buildings.

DMA decided to focus on the construction part of project delivery and further develop these skills within the practice. In the UK, Miller explains, architects who only work on the front end of projects often don't get to deliver the entire job. They reckoned that a strong reputation around delivery and construction would provide economic stability for the practice, but would also mean they were more likely to be involved with the full construction process. A main objective of this strategy was to consider the construction process and workflows, and how to best maintain a high degree of quality throughout the entire design process. As Miller explains, 'If you design a building, there is nothing more frustrating than seeing it delivered to a lower quality than you know was possible. We felt it was important to start from this.'

Another important characteristic of the practice is their open, collaborative approach. Miller explains, 'We realised there were opportunities for less adversarial and more collaborative relationships with engineers, contractors and fabricators, and this is a fundamental aspect of the way that we work. We use technology as an enabler in this and, by sharing our data-rich 3D models, we are able to develop our designs together with our clients, consultants, contractors and suppliers, as well as planners and other stakeholders.' This has helped the practice to develop a new market, and has led to a new kind of client. In recent years, contracting companies have become more and more involved in project development, in order to fund projects that they then build. Miller further explains, 'These companies operate by moving around money and become partners in projects in early stages. As they are contractors by nature, they choose their design team based on the premise that the design team is great also in the later phases of the construction project.'

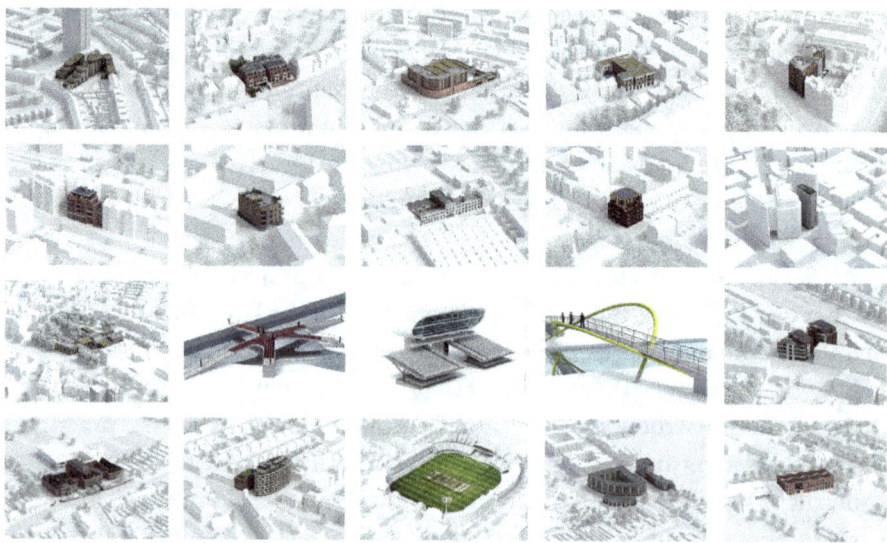

Figure 37.5.1 *Projects by David Miller Architects.*

Miller explains that the practice does not have a marketing strategy, but that there is a massive marketing effort, be it slightly different to mainstream marketing methodology. The practice is not often in the press, but instead they invest a lot of time in conferences, and, over the last eight years, they have presented at over 250 events in the technical arena, speaking the language of this discipline. Miller says, 'Architects sometimes don't fully embrace that we are part of the wider construction industry. It's very nice to build a gallery in Tuscany, but 95% of what we do involves more everyday typologies; we build schools and hospitals and housing.'

The practice is also committed to making sure they are a responsible business, putting social value and inclusivity at the heart of what they do. They put a lot of energy into activities that help to build sustainable communities, assisting and supporting other local businesses, often giving their time pro-bono, and encouraging and supporting a wide range of young people into the industry through partnerships with schools, local authorities and charitable organisations. Miller's business partner, Fiona Clark, often speaks about these activities at conferences and, in doing so, addresses potential clients such as councils and housing associations, who are also enthusiastic about creating social value. Clark strongly believes that this approach gives back as much as it takes and that would seem to be the case, since they have a laudable 80% return clientele. Rather than adopting a conventional marketing strategy, it's a way of both marketing themselves and incrementally changing the profession and the industry for the better.

All this began with the unique selling points and a clear knowledge of what they are. 'We have a clear vision and strategy for the practice,' Miller explains. 'We know what we are here for. This vision goes through to processes and environments, and even to how the space that we work in reflects and supports our values and goals.' Their London office does indeed 'sell' the way that the practice works – it is a light, bright, linear slot of office space with one long desk and workstations along both sides. This means that there is no hierarchy and informal discussions about projects are a natural thing. The meeting tables are also part of the same space, so that clients feel they are part of the process and the knowledge spreads by 'osmosis'.

Miller maintains that it is important that their focus remains conceptual and content based. 'We see that people see our office interior as a best practice; it stands for peer-to-peer learning and collaborative working. Now that we are all tech workers, we try not to disappear into the computers and software but to nurture the social qualities of designing. We like to break down the division between the virtual realm and reality by learning and talking to each other, by putting up images of our work and by making many 3D models,' he explains.

The DMA website is different to other architects' websites. Its strong aesthetic features every project as a BIM model, which can be rotated and explored in section to interrogate the design. As Miller admits, it's a 'Marmite' website that doesn't necessarily appeal to everyone (especially not other architects!) but, as he explains, 'We don't sell to architects. Our clients understand it, and it seems to appeal to sophisticated technical clients such a construction firms and blue-chip clients. When we designed the website, we wanted to become known for BIM, but in a way that it would simply be recognised as our standard way of working, demonstrating how we work rather than having to talk about it.' The models that feature are the firm's construction models – they are the working 3D models that are used to design and build the buildings. This kind of communication is very much in line with the rational, technological, 'pared-back' approach of the firm. 'The models are honest and clear – they are not moody or artistic and there is no BMW in front of the front door. We are selling architecture, not a lifestyle,' says Miller.

As a small practice, DMA is fast, adaptable and agile. Where larger organisations might first need to gain approval from their board to train a large number of employees or to make larger investments for software licences, DMA have been able to remain a step ahead of their competitors. However, they don't see it as a competition. They are not a threat as a small organisation, and they are very keen to share their knowledge. A strong piece of marketing was the digital transformation they undertook within the practice, and how they endeavoured to learn about its financial feasibility. 'We monitored our efficiency and our cash flow and we shared this at conferences, so we could give evidence of how effective it was. We basically shared our turnover and our profit at these conferences in front of hundreds of people. Not being a threat and being different allowed us to do this,' Miller explains. This kind of openness secures a great deal of goodwill and support from larger organisations.

CASE STUDY 6
FEILDEN FOWLES – EDMUND FOWLES

'You have to be ready when an opportunity comes along; you have to seize it.'

Creating your own work.

Fergus Feilden and Edmund Fowles, of Feilden Fowles, were friends from their student days and share numerous interests and passions, having both been involved in building projects before joining the architecture school. In addition to a keen interest in architecture, they share interests in ecology and cycling. With this shared ethos, alongside their education, they designed their first project as a side job, an activity that they continued as they worked for other practices, to gain experience. This meant that the duo left university not only with a built reference, but also with the skillset of builders, something that many of their peers would only experience years later. 'Our passion and interest was always in making. We did not want to be paper architects, doing competition after competition. We are interested in the dirty end of architecture, the craftsmanship and being on site,' explains Fowles.

Their first client was a family friend and the project was a timber house in the Brecon Beacons, in Wales, built 2007–2009, before the practice was founded in 2009. As they had not yet graduated at the start of the project, they surrounded themselves with mentors and professionals who could help them complete the building.

After completion, marketing the project came naturally. They photographed the house, and got it published in the *Architects' Journal*. Their aim to receive awards for the building was impeded by the fact that they were not yet qualified architects, but they have made up for that since. This first project became a successful reference and allowed them to engage in the next projects. Clients understood that even in their early twenties they could be trusted with a budget.

The next few projects were smaller and less glamorous. 'As students we would read about the young post-war architects who built 5,000 homes as a first project. That's not happening anymore,' says Fowles. As they had ambition to expand their portfolio beyond residential design projects, they decided to create their own project by contacting Feilden's former school in Bath and offering them a £5,000 master plan for their new campus. The school grounds had many portacabins, having suffered from austerity measures. Feilden Fowles designed the master plan and helped them write applications for funding. They became friends of the school and soon began to create small projects in and around the campus, such as a covered walkway and outdoor classroom, all of which had an incremental impact on the site.

Eventually, the school needed a new learning centre with four classrooms, for which Feilden Fowles had written the brief in the master plan. The project came to tender and the two architects could not qualify due to a lack of relevant experience, so they found a larger practice to align with. They won the project, and this became a great success. To this day, they are key holder to the master plan and are already working on their fourth building on the site. The entire project reflects the way that the UK Government now distributes funding to schools via the Education Funding Authority. Rather than large sums of money to completely rebuild schools, such as the former Building Schools for the Future (BSF) scheme, funding comes in much smaller increments. Understanding this made their strategy an intelligent one. Additional educational projects followed on the heels of the first, and they soon expanded from primary and secondary schools to higher education.

Figure 37.6.1 *The temporary Feilden Fowles Studio in London, 2016.*

Another important milestone in the development of the practice was the Charlie Bigham's Food Production Campus. One of Bigham's children had been a student at a school realised by Feilden Fowles. Bigham admired the building and shortlisted Feilden Fowles as the wild card for a competition against some big names in architecture. They won (in 2015), and quickly learned about the scientific side of the food production process. They realised the building in a fast-track process, and made a 20-year master plan for the campus.

'With the cash flow generated by this larger-scale project, we were able to build our Waterloo studio, a temporary structure on land in London which we were initially allowed to use for five years,' says Fowles. The studio came about when two charities asked the young architects to make a plan for temporary use of part of an empty plot. Feilden Fowles offered a free master plan of the whole site in order to become fully involved in the project as a partner. 'I suppose this is some advice we received whilst studying: you have to be ready when an opportunity comes along; you have to seize it. As architects, you are so well placed to analyse the existing brief and you have the ability to turn it into something magic.'

This was only possible because this chain of events took place in the transition from one project to the next, giving them a critical cash flow and allowing them to build their own temporary studio in the middle of London. However, it is not entirely coincidental, as Feilden Fowles have a well-defined business plan, which they call the practice plan. In this plan is an ambition to grow by no more than two staff members a year, as this is beneficial to maintaining the culture of the practice, and as it facilitates the sustainable development of the practice. At just over a decade old, they have reached 20 people, all of which is according to plan.

The Waterloo studio was a pivotal moment for the practice, as it allowed them to demonstrate their values in terms of architecture, but also in terms of urban planning and their orientation to social issues. Building a temporary structure in economic terms was a break-even project compared to the rent the practice would have had to pay elsewhere, yet the real gain was in PR. 'We wanted to make the most of the potential press opportunities this unconventional studio and setting on an urban farm would allow,' explains Fowles. Part of the site is used for educational programmes, with a barn that doubles up to host a range of community and commercial events. As a member of the project, the architects get a few slots a year and were able to organise a RIBA summer party and a conference on sustainable construction. 'In creating this place, we wanted to bring as many people as we possibly could to the site, bring the audience to us, and it's been a really good opportunity to broaden the practice's PR.'

Feilden Fowles view PR as an important element for them in terms of growing the practice. They began with an in-house PR strategy document, which provided direction and served as a decision-making tool. Now the practice has a publicist, Claire Curtice Publicists. This was a large investment initially, but due to Curtice's personal approach, it was a highly valuable move. (Incidentally, Curtice responded quicker than any other architect or PR firm with respect to any image requests I made for this book.) 'Broadly our work with Claire covers areas like messaging, values and themes we want to talk about, such as crafts, education, various aspects of our current work and recently more about the arts,' explains Fowles. Also important was making investments in high-quality photography and the development of a professional website, as well as a clear presence on relevant social media channels. They align significant press moments with consistent information-sharing to maintain a continuous presence. 'The more proactive side is to go to events, giving talks that help shape the narrative of the practice, being on panels, opening up the studio for events and so on — PR is multifaceted,' says Fowles.

Figure 37.6.2 *Summer party at the Feilden Fowles Studio in London.*

Feilden Fowles view building openings as opportunities to invite existing clients and friends. These individuals have supported them in some way and, being movers and shakers, can potentially bring in new business. As such, their PR budget is around 5% of the practice's turnover.

Working abroad interests the practice, but there is one issue: in their practice plan, they forbid air travel, which is part of their philosophy to limit their impact on the planet. Their ambition is to purchase a piece of woodland in future where they can offset their CO_2 emissions and build a more radical, rural studio and workshop as a counterpart to their London studio.

Shaping all these ideas is a 'halo' of professional advisors. Fowles explains that it is important to know and understand your firm's weaknesses and when to seek help, rather than insisting on doing everything yourself. This philosophy serves them well, as the practice is just over a decade old, has a wonderfully consistent portfolio and an impressive range of awards, which includes reaching the final shortlist of the famed Stirling Prize.

CASE STUDY 7
TURNER WORKS – CARL TURNER

'There are smarter ways to win work than to participate in competitions.'

From architect to community builder.
Faced with the challenge of being relatively unknown but having skills and ambition, Carl Turner set out to design and build his own house, and decided to try his luck and call the Channel 4 TV show 'Grand Designs'. They accepted and started filming and following the construction process. 'It caused a great deal of stress being on TV with my own house. The pressure to do it well was obviously heavy,' says Turner. However, the project, completed in 2012, went well, won the Manser Medal and Turner quickly became a household name. 'Often when I went to events, strangers started talking to me, and I had to ask them whether we had met before. It turned out that they had seen me on TV. It put my name and my face together. To many people, my TV presence was almost like an endorsement, that I was a trustworthy person.'

Though some may claim it's a dying medium, the power of television is undeniable, and its potential reach spectacular. During the construction project and in more recent television appearances on another Channel 4 television show, 'Ugly House to Lovely House', Turner presented himself as a great listener, as opposed to the stereotypical arrogant architect. He also turned out to be the only architect able to work within budget. Again, this was great PR.

Television creates instant fame, but while Turner's commissions increased, these were requests to create the same house for other clients. Larger and more complex commissions never materialised. To address this, he hired a communications specialist to help him develop a strategy to change the public's perception of him as an architect exclusively designing single-family homes. The communications specialist advised him to engage in public debate and to become an industry thought leader. To do this, he pitched for the RIBA Council, one of a number of platforms where he could talk about his passions, such as social values and community building, or the issue of gentrification versus regeneration. Mentoring and training for young architects is also one of his priorities, and addressing the fact that architecture is an increasingly middle-class profession due to limited social mobility.

'It sounds almost cynical but it isn't; it's a strategic way to think about a career, defining the position you have, and defining a goal where you want to be,' Turner explains. This transformed how the practice works. 'So we developed this idea of self-initiated projects. There are smarter ways to win work than to participate in competitions.'

Practically, it meant that Carl Turner Architects rebranded itself as Turner Works in 2017, dropping the word 'Architecture', to support the new focus of the practice. 'Architecture is, in a way, linked to developers and gentrification; it would not work in the field in which we are now active. In this field, it has a bad connotation,' says Turner. Turner Works are quite unusual in what they do. There are four main elements and architecture is just one: imagining, designing, making and running. 'We do lots of micro plans instead of master plans. For example, for New Haven, we analyse the town and imagine fast micro projects that will change the town immediately, and not only after two decades of construction whilst investing millions.'

Figure 37.7.1 *The Community Hall at The Coachworks, Ashford, Kent, Turner Works, 2019.*

One of their most successful projects is Pop Brixton, a new mini-city of culture, enterprise and community. 'We developed this expertise in meanwhile spaces, temporary projects. At the time, I lived in Brixton and the council advertised, looking for initiatives for a site. They were searching for people with ideas, people to realise them and to run the project. I sold my house and invested into the project. I basically became a community developer,' Turner says. POP Brixton is a great success, attracting over a million visitors a year. Being an architect and not an operator, Turner established the entire operation, transformed it into a business and then stepped back from it. However, the business model forced him to venture into becoming a contractor. If he had not done this, costs would have been crippling.

In addition to traditional typologies of housing and public buildings, Turner Works now have expertise in creating meanwhile spaces. 'My job in the practice is to be the face of the practice and to network and bring in the new work. I am in charge of the future. Up to a certain point I am also still the creative director, but on a larger scale,' explains Turner.

Because Turner is both an architect and an entrepreneur, he was able to develop another initiative in which he helped establish the company Make Shift, which not only runs Pop Brixton, but also Hackney Bridge and Peckham Levels, all of which were designed by Turner Works. With this company backed by investors, he created a client for Turner Works. 'We basically founded our own client. It's great for us, but also for them because I bring the experience of these projects to the table. I am an architect who understands the business model. It's important for architects to be sympathetic with a client's business model,' says Turner.

Due to this speciality, clients now approach him directly. For example, the borough council of Ashford, in Kent, wanted to turn their commercial quarter into a meanwhile destination. Turner Works did the design and contracting for The Coachworks, completed in 2019, and will run the operation for at least five years. The council, which invested in the construction and owns the land, receives 15% of the profit, which makes it less risky as a business model. In the end, Turner will be handing it over to a third party, involved only from a distance.

Having this niche is a great business proposition. 'We are really unusual. We are solving the problems for councils, but there are not that many people out there who can do it. We created a very special niche for ourselves. If we can't find someone else, we operate the site, but being architects, we prefer to establish a new company and make it independent from us,' he explains. 'Our holy grail and marketing strategy is to become an expert in a few specialisms which will bring work to us and will open doors. We are the place-makers, the zero-to-three-year people. We are the people who populate the site and find local talent that can inform what the final development could be, because in the temporary project phase we can analyse the demand on the site.'

Figure 37.7.2 *POP Brixton, Turner Works, 2015.*

Turner also does the more traditional marketing, pitching, competitions and PR, but Turner Works' main attraction is the expertise in their niche. Temporary projects generate new work. The reference Pop Brixton, for example, got him the commission to design an arts academy, Mountview Academy, in Peckham, London, a 10,000m2 cultural building completed in 2018. 'We went from delivering a few private houses to Pop Brixton and then to a public building, the Mountview Academy. The drama school people visited us in Pop Brixton and were impressed. It opened a new typology for us,' says Turner.

However, the niche is not everything. It was important to diversify from only being the meanwhile architect. This would probably allow them to win more work, so diversifying was a deliberate decision – and a more ambitious one. Staff and partners did not want to be typecast.

Having been on television, Turner understands the effect of PR. He finds this especially crucial in community projects, so each project has its own website and social media profile. At the practice, they work with blogs, guided tours and making space for the projects to speak for themselves by organising targeted meetings and events on site. Turner believes that they have never gained new projects from publications in architecture magazines.

Temporary projects need a certain aesthetic, and so the renders by Turner Works are suited to the programme. To this end, in the meanwhile spaces a cool collage style works very well. This informal and young style is relevant to the target group that will use the spaces later. In this way, the graphics lend themselves to a holistic PR approach.

Sharing knowledge and learning from others is not an empty phrase for Turner, who spends up to 20% of his time doing speculative work, thinking about the practice, lecturing, teaching and investing into the discipline. This creates new ideas: for example, the London Practice Forum, in which 25 emerging practices exchange ideas with each other and consider co-locating to behave like swarm offices that share amenities and services while each maintaining their own identity. 'It might never happen, but it's a great idea to further discuss and who knows what will come out of it,' says Turner.

CASE STUDY 8
POWERHOUSE COMPANY – NANNE DE RU

'Our goal is to have 100% control over the entire process.'

From 0 to 100 staff in 15 years.

Powerhouse was founded in 2005 when the young practice impressed the world with a widely published villa and intriguing research projects. The practice weathered the financial crisis of 2008 and excelled, launching into the commercial market with sizable projects. Today, the 100-staff practice features a technical architecture office, PCCE, and RED Company, a project development company they launched in 2015.

The transformation from niche architecture firm to a sizable commercial practice was mobilised following an evaluation of the economic side of architecture. Frustrated by projects being cancelled during the global economic crisis in 2008, Nanne de Ru and historian Hans Ibelings undertook a social-critical study drawing a connection between architecture and the economy. This led to the insight that 'a sound understanding of the world of money is absolutely essential if you want to create buildings'.

He realised that if he wanted to build buildings, have financial stability, pay adequate wages to his staff and be relevant, he needed to support a company of a certain scale. It isn't that working on a villa is less compelling than a larger project, but there is an economic difference. With just three large projects, you can sustain an office. With three villas, this is difficult. De Ru began to perceive the missing link in the market – the full-service architect. This entity was something that had become a rarity in the Netherlands, as universities and technical universities have established an apartheid between two kinds of architects: the conceptualist and the technical architect.

Uniting the two became a business model and the wish to be a sizable office led to innovative ways to realise this. De Ru lobbied project developers and construction companies. His first success with a construction company was an office building executed in full service for Heijmans. As one of the most renowned Dutch construction companies, this raised some eyebrows, and it became clear to potential clients that if he could realise technical drawings for Heijmans, Powerhouse's technical architecture arm had professional credibility.

Convincing project developers was far more daunting, but De Ru also found a solution for this. Whenever he would find a client willing to work with him but sceptical of his abilities, he would form an alliance with an even larger office. A personal click with the principals was conditional, and for the larger office, this offered a fresh perspective, so the prospect of a collaborative project was convincing. In this way, Powerhouse were able to punch above their weight and realise a series of large projects. This was all while being a young firm without the required references, in the midst of an economic crisis that crippled many established firms.

This was not always easy, and sometimes for the sake of turnover, and growth, the practice realised projects they would not publish on their website. De Ru made an honest analysis – he thinks that architects focus on turning any project into a masterpiece and so sometimes they lose sight of their client's ambitions and strive for something impossible. In this way, he accepts collateral damage in terms of aesthetic quality for the greater good of the company.

In 2012, Powerhouse Company separated from its technical arm and founded a separate entity that works for third parties. However, the next essential business innovation occurred in 2015 with the launch of RED Company. This emerged from frustration about operating in a black box when working with developers. Growing tired of not understanding the

Figure 37.8.1 *The ASICS EMEA Headquarters by Powerhouse Company, Hoofddorp, the Netherlands, 2016–19.*

business model for his projects, and having no insight into costs and profits, he was puzzled by the difference in income between architects and developers. Therefore, De Ru decided to learn how to develop, first with small projects and later with serious and sizable developments. He says, 'The start was labour intensive because we had no money to invest ourselves, but we learned a lot. If you really want to be in control over your projects this is the way to gain total control. Our goal is to have 100% control over the entire process.'

When I asked him if his existing clients viewed him as competition, he agrees that this was a concern in the beginning, but he believes there is now understanding of the benefits. De Ru says that Powerhouse's 'commercial clients want to have a handsome building, but in addition they also want to have efficient layouts and a decent technical story. Being my own project developer and client, I learned how to become a much better commercial architect.' This not only adds value on the design side, but also in terms of understanding the entire process. This made it easier to mitigate between the different interests within the construction team. De Ru compares this to working in the 1930s, when the industrial age demanded innovation from architects. This is his way of dealing with the capitalist age, and generating innovations.

The next step to gaining 100% control through design is through the management of the entire construction process by establishing a construction management company. After controlling finances, this next step will control and facilitate execution, and ultimately quality in terms of materialisation. In this way, Powerhouse Company has come full circle from their first project, Villa One, which was entirely designed and delivered by De Ru, on time and on budget. This holistic process returns 15 years later with larger, more complex executions.

De Ru shares this advice with young architects, 'Don't forget that there is a different perception in architecture. Try to see things from a different perspective. And work hard, because it brings success and happiness.'

ACKNOWLEDGEMENTS

THANKS TO...
Amanda Rooseboom (MVRDV) for her never-ending patience and support organising my schedule.
Antonio Luca Coco (MVRDV) for his priceless help with the renders.
Carl Turner (Turner Works) for showing how architects can transform themselves.
Christiane Bürklein (MVRDV) for proofreading and removing the 'skinny white male' overload.
Clare Holloway (RIBA) for her incredible support in making this book and her critical comments. Writing a book with such a support system is amazing.
David Miller (DMA) for sharing his special technological niche.
Edmund Fowles (Feilden Fowles) for sharing his insight into seizing business opportunities.
Elizabeth Webster (RIBA) for her great support and taking over during the lockdown. Any silly question by me was answered immediately.
Hazel Rounding (shedkm) for sharing her view on architecture and business.
Helen Castle (RIBA) for initiating this book and supporting me by challenging me to think even harder about my work.
Inger Kammeraat (MVRDV) for proofreading and softening my rough edges.
Irene Start (MVRDV) for proofreading the PR part.
James Crawford (Studio MUTT) for sharing his wonderful experience on how to become famous on Instagram.
Jessica Cullen (MVRDV) for her massive and daunting task of changing my 'Denglish' (a mix of Dutch or Deutsch (German) and English) into a proper English, while maintaining the tone and bite of the texts.
Lachlan Anderson-Frank (Lichfields) for proofreading the PR part.
Malcolm Reading (Malcolm Reading Consultants) for his generous advice to architects.
Mariana Idiarte (Mariana Idiarte Business Consultant) for proofreading the sections on contracts, fee proposals and legal procedures.
Mathew Giles and Matthew Ashton (MgMaStudio) for their inspiring account of growth in crisis times.
Miruna Dunu (MVRDV) for her precious help with the diagrams.
My family for their never-ending love, care and patience.
Nanne de Ru (Powerhouse Company) for his strategic explanation of how to become a sizable office.
Oana Rades and Harm Timmermans (Shift A+U) for always questioning my advice and hence challenging me.
Phil Coffey (Coffey Architects) for sharing his business insight and his ethos.
Suzanne van der Pluijm (MVRDV) for helping to organise and looking for images; it was a tough job because many practices don't reply to such a request or demand access to the text or ask for high fees.
Suzy Jones (RIBA North) for finding the right interview partners in Liverpool.
V8 Architects for sharing their great story of growing their practice.
Winy, Jacob and Nathalie (MVRDV) for allowing me to write this book. As we became more media savvy in the late 2000s, they kept inviting architect-friends for fast sessions with me to explain how PR works; this made me work on lectures and on sharing my knowledge.

Without the kind support of all these people, this book would not have been possible.

IMAGE CREDITS

FIGURE 0.1	Shift A+U
FIGURE 0.2	MVRDV
FIGURE 1.1	MLBS
FIGURE 3.1	Rob 't Hart / MVRDV
FIGURE 3.2	Markus Bredt
FIGURE 6.1	MVRDV
FIGURE 7.1.1	Strategizer.com
FIGURE 8.1	Ossip van Duivenbode / MVRDV
FIGURE 10.5.1	Wahyu Pratomo & Kris Provoost
FIGURE 10.6.1	Ossip van Duivenbode / MVRDV
FIGURE 10.6.2	MVRDV
FIGURE 10.6.3	MVRDV
FIGURE 11.1	MVRDV
FIGURE 13.1.1	MVRDV
FIGURE 13.1.2	MVRDV
FIGURE 13.1.3	MVRDV
FIGURE 13.1.4	MVRDV / Provast
FIGURE 13.2.1	MVRDV
FIGURE 13.2.2	MVRDV
FIGURE 13.2.3	MVRDV
FIGURE 13.2.4	MVRDV
FIGURE 13.2.5	MVRDV
FIGURE 13.2.6	MVRDV
FIGURE 13.2.7	MVRDV / Luxigon
FIGURE 13.2.8	MVRDV / Luxigon
FIGURE 13.2.9	MVRDV / Luxigon
FIGURE 13.2.10	MVRDV
FIGURE 13.3.1	MVRDV
FIGURE 13.3.2	WORKac
FIGURE 13.3.3	Foster + Partners
FIGURE 13.3.4	Foster + Partners
FIGURE 13.3.5	Turner Works
FIGURE 13.5.1	MVRDV
FIGURE 14.1	Rob 't Hart / MVRDV
FIGURE 16.1	MVRDV
FIGURE 19.1	MVRDV
FIGURE 20.1	Goethe - public domain
FIGURE 21.1	V8 Architects
FIGURE 22.1	MVRDV
FIGURE 22.2	MVRDV
FIGURE 23.1	MVRDV
FIGURE 23.2	MVRDV
FIGURE 24.1	Hamburg Marketing / Maxim Schulz
FIGURE 26.1	PLP Architects
FIGURE 31.1	RIBA
FIGURE 33.1	MVRDV
FIGURE 36.1	Bernardo Schuhmacher / BIG
FIGURE 37.1.1	shedkm
FIGURE 37.2.1	MgMaStudio
FIGURE 37.2.2	MgMaStudio
FIGURE 37.3.1	Studio Mutt
FIGURE 37.4.1	Coffey Architects
FIGURE 37.4.2	Coffey Architects
FIGURE 37.5.1	David Miller Architects
FIGURE 37.6.1	Feilden Fowles
FIGURE 37.6.2	Feilden Fowles
FIGURE 37.7.1	Turner Works
FIGURE 37.7.2	Turner Works
FIGURE 37.8.1	Powerhouse Company

INDEX

A
abstract models 88
advertising 36, 57, 74, 76
advice 153–5
agents 114
appointments *see* contracts
'archispeak' 84–5
architectural awards 64–5
architectural styles 156–8
augmented reality 89
awards 64–5

B
brand magazines 38
branding 17–19, 88
brochures 126
building openings 91–2
buildings tours 92–3
built project 91–4
business cards 17
business development 22, 106–7, 115–16
Business Model Canvas (BMC) 25
business plan 26

C
case studies
  Coffey Architects 181–4
  DMA 186–8
  Feilden Fowles 189–93
  MgMaStudio 173–6
  Powerhouse 199–201
  shedkm 170–2
  Studio MUTT 177–80
  Turner Works 194–8
client characteristics 112–14
client relationships 94, 108–11
collaboration 11, 146, 150–2
collages 79–81, 84
commissions 106–7, 145

communication skills 58, 84–7, 143 (*see also* presentation skills)
company culture 19
competition books 96–7
competitions 1–2, 3, 71
completion date 94
contacts 39, 94, 143 (*see also* networking)
contracts 121, 132–6, 152
controversy *see* crises
corporate identity 17–19
crises 51–7, 165–7

D
design liability 135
digital media 34
domestic projects 108, 145
drawings 66–70
dress code 19

E
elevator pitch 15, 57
energy-efficient design 137
environmental sustainability 137–40
ethics 159–61
exclusivity requirements 39
executive architects 151
exhibition stands 125
exhibitions 98–101

F
facebook 42–3, 44
fairs 123–6
fee proposals 121, 127–31
film clips 49–50
fraud 164

G
Google Alerts 33
Google Analytics 32, 33
graphic design 17–18, 30
green buildings 137–40

H
hand drawings 81, 83, 84

I
instagram 42, 44
insurance 135
intellectual property rights 133, 135–6
international collaboration 150
intranets 57
invoicing 130

J
job advertisements 57
joint ventures 152
journalists 37, 38, 39

L
language 84–7, 143
lectures 58–63, 125
legal action 162–3
liability in contract 135
licenses 135
LinkedIn 42, 44
local media 38
local participation *see* public participation

M
magazines 37
marketing 13
marketing strategy 24–6
media 34, 36–9
media analytics 32, 33
media training 47
mentors 155
mission statements 14–16, 140
mixed-use projects 146
models 88–90

N

negotiations 129, 132, 133, 134
neighbours *see* public participation
networking 123, 153–5
  (*see also* contacts)
news media 36–7

O

office design and management 27–9
online media 34, 40–2
  (*see also* social media; website design)
opening parties 91–2
openings 91–2
overseas partners 120
overseas work 64, 117–22
cultural differences 110, 121
ethical considerations 160
international collaborations 150
PR 43
rules and regulations 136

P

partnerships 146, 150
past clients 94
payment 130
lectures 61
withheld 135, 162
personal presentation 19, 143
personal qualities 112
photorealistic render *see* render
Photoshop 74
physical models 88–9, 90
pitches *see* presentations
planning workflow 147–9
podcasts 49–51
portfolio building 145–6
post-occupancy visits 92–3
PR agencies 38, 103
practice management
office premises 27–9

workflow 147–9
practice size 145
presentation skills 61–2
presentations 12, 125, 141–4
press releases 85, 86–7
print media 36–9
prioritising 102–3
private residences *see* domestic projects
professional advice 153–5
professional ethics 159–61
project book 95–7
project completion 94
project teams 151–2
project texts 85–6
public clients 113, 139
public events *see* exhibitions; fairs
public participation 52–3, 55, 57, 84, 85–6, 91
public relations 22–4, 34–6, 51–7
public speaking 58–63, 61–2, 125
public tenders 106, 146
public voting 65
publicity 15, 35–6

R

render 71–9
render studios 74, 76
resource planning 147–9

S

sales approach 114
'sales' drawings 67
sales pitch 15, 57
self-publishing 41
site visits 91
sketches *see* hand drawings
social media 42–6
social media storms 52, 54–5
spam 164
specialisation 8–12 (*see also* typologies)
staff development 149

staff management 147
staff pay and benefits 6–7
standard contracts 132–3, 134
styles of architecture 156–8
suing the client 162–3
sustainability 137–40

T

television 46–8
tender procedures 12
tenders 106, 115
3D models 89, 90
TikToc 49, 50
tours 92–3
trade fairs 123–6
travel costs 131
Twitter 39, 42, 44
typologies 8–9, 145–6 (*see also* specialisation)

U

unique selling point 26, 118–19
unpaid work 3–4
urban planning 149

V

video clips 49–50
Vimeo 49, 50
virtual reality 89
vision statements 14–16
visualisation drawings *see* design visualisation
vlogs 49–51

W

web designers 33
website 30–3
workflow 147–9
written communication 84–7

Y

youTube 46–7, 49, 50, 51

ENDNOTES

CHAPTER 1
1. L. Fessler, 6 February 2018, 'Architecture's biggest CEO gets her business advice from the Joker', https://qz.com/work/1176090/big-ceo-sheela-maini-sogaard-gets-her-business-advice-from-the-joker

CHAPTER 2
1. M. Riscica, 24 March 2014, '10 reasons why you SHOULD NOT become an architect', Youngarchitect.com
2. I. Block, 25 March 2019, 'Architects who don't pay interns "shouldn't be given prestigious commissions" says designer who revealed Ishigami internships', www.dezeen.com/2019/03/25/architects-unpaid-internship-serpentine-pavilion/#:~:text=Architects%20who%20rely%20on%20free,boil%2C%22%20Furman%20told%20Dezeen

CHAPTER 4
1. Z. Williams, 2020, 'Marketing to architects: The definitive guide to selling architects', www.venveo.com/blog/marketing-to-architects

CHAPTER 7
1. L. O'Connell, 9 August 2019, 'Nike's marketing expenses worldwide from 2014 to 2019', www.statista.com/statistics/685734/nike-ad-spend
2. B. Colomina, 1994, 'Mies Not', in *The Presence of Mies*, D. Mertens (ed), Princeton Architectural Press, New York
3. A. Osterwalder and Y. Pigneur, 2010, *Business Model Generation*, Wiley, Hoboken, New Jersey

CHAPTER 9
1. herzogdemeuron.com; zaha-hadid.com

CHAPTER 10
1. H. Muschamp, 7 September 1997, 'The Miracle in Bilbao', *The New York Times*
2. www.nctj.com/downloadlibrary/JaW%20Report%202018.pdf
www.prca.org.uk/sites/default/files/PR%20and%20Communications%20Census%202018.pdf
3. www.villamedia.nl/artikel/18.000-journalisten-in-nederland; www.adformatie.nl/carriere/nationaal-onderzoek-aantal-communicatieprofessionals-nl
4. Statistica research department, 3 May 2016, 'Online video viewing penetration among internet users worldwide as of 1st quarter 2016, by age group', www.statista.com/statistics/272935/share-of-consumers-who-watch-online-video-by-age
5. M. Chatel, 14 July 2016, 'The Top 12 architecture channels on YouTube', www.archdaily.com/791306/the-top-12-architecture-channels-on-youtube
6. www.mvrdv.nl/projects/10/depot-boijmans-van-beuningen
7. www.mvrdv.nl/news/385/mvrdv-designs-thecloud-two-connected-luxury-residential-towersin-seoul-korea
8. MVRDV and 120 architects, ZAC Bastide Niel, www.bastideniel.fr

CHAPTER 13
1. www.forbes.com/sites/forbesagencycouncil/2017/08/25/finding-brand-success-in-the-digital-world

CHAPTER 13
1. J. Knikker, 1 October 2015, 'MVRDV's Markthal PR campaign; or, How we learned the price of chicken', www.archdaily.com/774612/mvrdvs-markthal-prcampaign-or-how-we-learned-the-price-of-chicken

CHAPTER 22
1. I. Lalueta, 20 November 2014, 'The "average" architect's salary in the world', *Metalocus*

CHAPTER 24
1. C. Rickens, 7 February 2013, 'Pannenprojekt: Elbphilharmonie-Architekten kassieren mehr als 90 Millionen Euro', *Der Spiegel*, www.spiegel.de/wirtschaft/soziales/elbphilharmonie-architekten-kassieren-mehr-als-90-millionen-euro-a-881056.html

CHAPTER 26
1. Snohetta.com, 29 November 2019, 'An ambitious journey ahead', https://snohetta.com/news/462-an-ambitious-journey-ahead
2. www.breeam.com

CHAPTER 27
1. Archinect, 19 November 2012, 'Watch Koolhaas, Hadid, Rogers Stirk Harbour and Foster pitch their proposals for the new L&L Tower', https://archinect.com/news/article/61718170/watch-koolhaas-hadid-rogers-stirk-harbour-and-foster-pitch-their-proposals-for-the-new-l-l-tower
2. O. Wainwright, 19 November 2012, 'Pitch battle: watch four star architects compete to design New York tower', *The Guardian*, www.theguardian.com/artanddesign/architecture-design-blog/2012/nov/19/architects-zaha-hadid-norman-foster

CHAPTER 28
1. 'Architectural Practices', Constructuk.com, directory/category
2. www.academics.de/ratgeber/architekt-gehalt

CHAPTER 32
1. M. Kushner, March 2014, 'Why the buildings of the future will be shaped by you', https://www.ted.com/talks/marc_kushner_why_the_buildings_of_the_future_will_be_shaped_by_you/transcript?language=en

CHAPTER 33
1. D. Sudjic, 2005, *The Edifice Complex: How the Rich and Powerful Shape the World*, Allen Lane, London
2. I. Buruma, 30 July 2002, 'Don't be fooled – China is not squeaky clean', *The Guardian*, www.theguardian.com/world/2002/jul/30/china.features11

For Product Safety Concerns and Information please contact our EU
representative GPSR@taylorandfrancis.com
Taylor & Francis Verlag GmbH, Kaufingerstraße 24, 80331 München, Germany

www.ingramcontent.com/pod-product-compliance
Lightning Source LLC
Chambersburg PA
CBHW070607300426
44113CB00010B/1438